C000124821

The Oedipus Complex

A Selection of Classic
Articles on Sigmund
Freud's Psychoanalytical
Theory

By

Various Authors

Copyright © 2011 Read Books Ltd.
This book is copyright and may not be
reproduced or copied in any way without
the express permission of the publisher in writing

British Library Cataloguing-in-Publication Data
A catalogue record for this book is available from
the British Library

Sigmund Freud

Sigismund Schlomo Freud was born on 6th May 1856, in the Moravian town of Příbor, now part of the Czech Republic.

Sigmund was the eldest of eight children to Jewish Galician parents, Jacob and Amalia Freud. After Freud's father lost his business as a result of the Panic of 1857, the family were forced to move to Leipzig and then Vienna to avoid poverty. It was in Vienna that the nine-year-old Sigmund enrolled at the Leopoldstädter Kommunal-Realgymnasium before beginning his medical training at the University of Vienna in 1873, at the age of just 17. He studied a variety of subjects, including philosophy, physiology, and zoology, graduating with an MD in 1881.

The following year, Freud began his medical career in Theodor Meynert's psychiatric clinic at the Vienna General Hospital. He worked there until 1886 when he set up in private practice and began specialising in "nervous disorders". In the same year he married Merth Bernays, with whom he had 6 children between 1887 and 1895.

In the period between 1896 and 1901, Freud isolated himself from his colleagues and began work on developing the basics of his psychoanalytic theory. He published *The Interpretation of Dreams*, in 1899, to a lacklustre reception, but continued to produce works such as *The Psychopathology of Everyday Life* (1901) and *Three Essays on the Theory of Sexuality* (1905). He held a weekly meeting at his home known as the "Wednesday Psychological Society" which eventually developed into the Vienna Psycho-Analytic Society. His ideas gained momentum and by the end of the decade his methods were being used internationally by neurologists and psychiatrists.

Freud made a huge and lasting contribution to the field of psychology with many of his methods still being used in modern psychoanalysis. He inspired much discussion on the wealth of theories he produced and the reactions to his works began a century of great psychological investigation.

In 1930 Freud fled Vienna due to rise of Nazism and resided in England until his death from mouth cancer on 23rd September 1939.

Contents

THE OEDIPUS COMPLEX

The latent influence on normal persons; its negative manifestations in the psychoneuroses and psychoses

Of the many interesting and valuable discoveries furnished to us through psychoanalysis none is as important as those facts which treat of the individual's relation to the family and society. In our psychoanalytic work with patients we find that parents play the leading part in their infantile psychic life. This fact is so universal and important that we may say that unless it is thoroughly elaborated and discussed with the patient no analysis is complete or effective. Studies made of psychoneurotics amply demonstrate that contrary to the accepted opinions neurotics are only exaggerations of the normal and that the modes of reaction in both are about the same. The only difference lies in the fact that one can adjust himself to his environments while the other finds it difficult or impossible to do so. If one should ask wherein these difficulties lie the experienced psychoanalyst would readily point to the parents. Indeed the more we study the psychoneuroses and the psychoses the clearer it becomes that the most potent factor in their determination is the early parental influence. That our parents should play a leading part in our lives is so obvious that it hardly needs further discussion. The strange part of it, however, is the fact that these relations are not as amicable or peaceful as seems at first sight. What I mean to say is that, contrary to general belief, there is usually not much love lost between parents and children and that especially little children do not always love their parents in a manner generally accepted. On the contrary they often show a marked dislike especially for one of their parents. This statement may sound very bold and unfounded, but if you will stop to think for a moment you will soon feel that it strikes a familiar note. Observation teaches that our love for parents is not innate and spontaneous and that it follows the same laws as that among strangers. Although Freud gave us the true psychological explanation of this conception the principle of it must have been known from time immemorial. History and every-day life demonstrate it. We all know the fifth commandment: Honor thy father and thy mother, that thy days may be long in the land which the Lord thy God giveth thee. Here we have a direct order to honor our parents and judging by the other commandments and by our modern laws, it must be concluded that to neglect parents was just as natural in the Biblical times as were those impulses against which commandments beginning with "Thou shalt not" had to be imposed. For it is a fact that there is no necessity of commanding the individual to realize his impulses. Left to himself he would constantly try to realize them, and civilization, so called, simply consists of inhibitions imposed upon the individual by religion and society. The more one can inhibit his primitive impulses the more cultured he is, and savages and children must be taught inhibition to fit them

2

for society. To cite Freud: "A progressive renouncement of constitutional impulses, the activity of which afford the ego primary pleasure, seems to be one of the basic principles of human culture."[1] In brief, observation shows that parents are loved by children only when they deserve it, that is to say, when they do not interfere with the child's desires and above all when they give the child pleasure.

When we enter into the deeper mental mechanisms of our patients and investigate their love lives, we usually find that the little boy is more attached to his mother and the little girl to her father. In other words, the first woman a boy loves is his mother who forever remains as a model for his later selections of women. The little boy therefore finds his father in the way—he is his rival. When the father is not at home the little son has no one with whom to share his mother's affection. He is therefore angry at, and jealous of his father and often wishes him dead. The idea of death does not however, mean to the child what it means to the adult, it simply means to be away. One of my patients vividly recalls that at the age of four years he asked his mother whom she loved more him or his father, and when she said that she loved his father more he became furious and cried for hours. These infantile feelings of sex which later develop into adult sex lay the foundation for the symptoms appearing in the later neurosis. I could trace directly the symptoms of the cases that I have analyzed to such mechanisms. In normal persons we find the traces of this early love in the dreams of the death of near relatives especially the father.[2]

The sexual feeling for the mother and jealousy of the father is called by Freud the Oedipus complex because antiquity has furnished us with legendary material to confirm these facts. To put it in his words: "The deep and universal effectiveness of these legends can only be explained by granting a similar universal applicability to the above-mentioned assumption in infantile psychology."[3]

The legend referred to is the drama King Oedipus by Sophocles. In brief it reads as follows: Laius, the king of Thebes, married Jocasta. After years of childless marriage Laius visited the Delphian Apollo and prayed for a child. The answer of the god was as follows: "Your prayer has been heard and a son will be given to you, but you will die at his hand, for Zeus decided to fulfil the curse of Pelops whose son you have once kidnapped." In spite of the warning the son was born, but fearing the fulfilment of the oracle, the child's feet were pierced and tied, and delivered to a faithful servant to be exposed in the desert. The servant, however, gave the child to a Corinthian shepherd who took it to his master, King Polybus, who, being childless, adopted it and called it Oedipus, meaning swollen feet. When the boy grew up into manhood he became uncertain of his own origin and consulting the oracle received the following answer: "Beware that thou shouldst not murder thy father and marry thy mother." In order to avoid the fulfilment of this prophecy Oedipus at once left Corinth and accidentally wandered toward Thebes. On the way he met King Laius and struck him dead in an unexpected quarrel. He then came to the gates of Thebes where he solved the riddle of the Sphinx, driving the latter to suicide and thus freeing the city from a great scourge. As a reward for this he was elected king and presented with the hand of Jocasta, his mother. He reigned in peace for many

4

years and begot two sons and two daughters upon his unknown mother until a plague broke out which caused the
Thebans to consult the oracle. The messengers returned
with the advice that the plague would stop as soon as the
murderer of King Laius would be driven from the country.
Sophocles then develops the play in a psychoanalytic manner until the true relations are discovered, namely, that
Oedipus killed his father and married his own mother. The
drama ends by Oedipus blinding himself and wandering
away into voluntary exile.

In his characteristic penetrating way Freud draws
many interesting conclusions some of which I shall mention.
According to some commentators, Oedipus Tyrannus is a
tragedy of fate. Its tragic effect is said to be found in the
opposition between the powerful will of the gods and the
futile resistance of the human being who is threatened with
destruction. The tragedy teaches resignation to the will
of God and confession of one's own helplessness. This
tragedy has lately been revived by Max Reinhardt and
had a long and successful run in Berlin and London. From
what we have read, it would seem that it moves modern
men no less than it moved the contemporary Greek. In
our own times, however, one occasionally witnesses a play
dealing with the incest problem which is as tremendously
effective as the Greek drama. This seems to indicate that
the explanation of this fact cannot lie merely in the
assumption that the effect of the Greek tragedy is based upon
the opposition between human fate and human will,
but is to be sought in the peculiar nature of the material
by which the opposition is shown. There must be something in us which is prepared to recognize the compelling

power of fate in Oedipus while we justly condemn the situations occurring in tragedies of later date as arbitrary inventions. Witness, *e.g.*, the storm that has been produced in this country by Synge's Irish play "The Play-boy of the Western World," which is a veiled Oedipus complex. Freud states that there must be some unconscious factor corresponding to this inner voice, in the story of king Oedipus. "His fate moves us only for the reason that it might have been ours, for the oracle has· put the same curse upon us before our birth as upon him. Perhaps we are all destined to direct our first sexual impulses toward our mothers and our first hatred and violent wishes toward our father. Our dreams convince us of it. King Oedipus who killed his father and married his mother, is nothing but the realized wish of our childhood. But more fortunate than he we have since succeeded, unless we have become psychoneurotics, in withdrawing our sexual impulses from our mothers and in forgetting our jealousy of our fathers. We recoil from the person for whom this primitive wish has been fulfilled with all the force of the repression which these wishes have suffered within us. By his analysis showing us the guilt of Oedipus the poet urges us to recognize our own inner self, in which these impulses, even if repressed, are still present."

That the Oedipus legend originated in an extremely old dream material which deals with the painful disturbance of the relation toward one's own parents through the first impulses of sexuality, is unmistakably shown in the very text of Sophocles. Jocasta, comforting Oedipus, recalls to him the dream which is dreamed by so many people: "For, says she, it has already been the lot of many men

6

in dreams to think themselves partners of their mother's bed. But he passes most easily through life to whom those circumstances are trifles."[5] The dream of having sexual intercourse with one's own mother occurred at that time as it does to-day to many persons who tell it with indignation and astonishment. As may be understood, it is the key to the tragedy and the complement to the dream of the death of the father. The story of Oedipus is the reaction of the imagination to these two typical dreams and, just as the dream when occurring to an adult is experienced with feelings of resistance, so the legend must contain terror and self chastisement. An uncomprehending secondary elaboration tries to make it serve such theological purposes as mentioned above.

From my own experience I can fully corroborate Freud's claims. I have on record hundreds of dreams of sexual relations with one's own mother given to me by many patients. These dreams were usually quite plain and there was very little distortion to them. About half of these dreamers reported these dreams before they ever heard of any Oedipus complex, while the other half told about them after I had explained the mechanism. They all assured me that they were perfectly aware of these dreams and to my question why they had not told me before they invariably answered that it was too terrible and revolting a thing to tell, and that the only reason why they told them to me was because they were pleased to know they were not the only ones having such dreams. I can say the same of many women who dreamed that they had sexual relations with their fathers. I analyzed Oedipus dreams in which only the father or the mother was masked. Thus one of my female homosexuals told me that the only erotic dreams in which a man played a part was one of having had sexual intercourse with one of our Governors, but on associating to the dream, she told me that she was accustomed to refer to her father as the governor. As you know the president, governor and mayor in dreams usually means the father.[6]

Most of the Oedipus dreams, however, usually show a symbolization of the sexual act in which the parents may be quite plain. One of my patients dreamed that he climbed up a high water tower on a revolving staircase. On reaching midway he met his mother, who accompanied him to the top. The climbing became more and more difficult. He had to hold on very tightly to her for fear that they would both fall. They finally reached the top in a very exhausted state where they both laid down in bed together for a long rest. This patient slept with his mother until he was eighteen years old and, from his own admission, although he entertained no conscious sexual feelings toward her, he wished on at least a few occasions that he could marry her. To those acquainted with dream analysis this dream needs no further elucidation.[7]

A man of thirty-five years reported to me the following dream: "*I dreamt that I was in bed with my mother and as she was talking aloud I told her to be quiet as I was afraid that my father who was in the next room would hear us.*"

This patient was treated for psychosexual impotence and this dream came after unsuccessfully attempting heterosexual intercourse. He was his mother's favorite and owing to the fact that his father was a psychopathic individual who abused and terrified his family he hated him and was much attached to his mother. Whenever

8

his father went on a rampage his mother would lock herself in a room with him, and they often lived through in reality the experience described in the dream. This was also the reason for his sleeping with his mother up to the age of ten years. Disappointed in her husband she lavished all her affection on her son who supplied her with the love she craved. The patient stated that for years he was subject to nightmares showing almost the same content as the above-mentioned dream.

To understand the full significance of this dream it will be necessary to review a few psychological facts.

As stated above we are all destined to direct our first sexual impulses to our mothers. The first woman loved is one's own mother. It is the mother who impresses on the mind the woman-image which remains as a permanent standard for the female ideal. Normally a repression takes place and the boy gradually projects his love to strangers. Investigation shows that the love life of an individual begins at a very early age and as this progresses the love for one's mother gradually fades from consciousness. In the unconscious it remains forever and acts as a constant guide in the future selection of a woman.[8] Every woman in compared to the mother-image and *cæteris paribus*, the closer the resemblance to the stronger the woman attracts us. This may shade from the normal to the abnormal. As examples I can cite the following cases:

A very cultured man was attracted only by very stout servants. No other type of woman appealed to him. Analysis showed that his first sexual impulses were aroused by a servant girl of that type who took the place of his mother.

A refined married woman of twenty-four years suffered from psychosexual frigidity, but was sexually excited whenever she saw a lame man. This was due to an identification with her mother who had an illicit love affair with a man when she was three or four years old. Like a great many grown-ups her mother considered her little girl an unthinking being and took no pains to conceal anything from her. When her paramour sustained a fracture of his leg and she found it necessary to make frequent calls on him she took her little daughter with her so as to avoid gossip. Although what she witnessed apparently made no impression on her at the time it nevertheless acted as a sexual trauma and formed an association between sex and lameness. This was also determined by the fact that at a later age this lame man took the place of her own father by marrying her widowed mother.

A young married woman who is dominated by a veritable prostitution complex carried on illicit relations with men while she lived with her husband. Psychoanalysis showed that she was an only daughter and although her father's pet she saw very little of him during her early childhood as his affairs took him away from home. As far as her memory reached she recalled witnessing unholy loves between her mother and "strange men." She herself married a man who not only belongs to the same type as her father, but who even follows her father's vocation. She thus identified herself with her mother in every respect.

Many of the unhappy love affairs and marriages are determined by such unconscious factors. Thus a very cultured woman of thirty-four was particularly interested in reforming criminals of a certain type. In her efforts to do good she made the acquaintance of a man recently discharged from prison who claimed that his downfall was due to drink. This acquaintanceship ripened into friendship and finally this ordinary ex-convict was bold enough to propose marriage. Although all her friends and relatives were shocked at the very idea of her marrying this man, she could only reject him after much struggle whereupon he began to drink. As soon as she heard of it she at once assured him of her love and promised to marry him. No sooner done than she immediately felt that she made a great mistake, that she really did not love the man, that she was only interested in reforming him. She broke the engagement but as soon as she heard that he was again drinking she again hastened to assure him that she would marry him. These episodes repeated themselves many times; when he was sober she could never think of him as a husband but as soon as he became drunk she could hardly resist him. When her friends brought her to me I discovered that this man unconsciously represented her own father who though cultured and refined died a drunkard.

I could quote many more cases,* but these will suffice to show the unconscious parental influence. Such influences are found in every person and although they are usually quite harmless they sometimes act perniciously. This is particularly true of only or favorite children who are overburdened with love. They are not allowed to follow the different stages of the psychosexual evolution and their libido remains fixed on the mother.[10] The result of such a process may be psychosexual impotence. By

* Most of the cases described by Mantegazzo as Idiogamists probably belong to this category; Zeitschrift J. Sexualwissenschaft. p. 223.

preventing the boy from projecting his love to strangers there results an unconscious incestuous fixation on the mother which then acts as an inhibition to sexual relations with other women.[11]

Let us return to the above-mentioned dream. From what we know of dreams we may say that those which are accompanied by fear are of a gross sexual nature. The fear as was said above, is the converted libido and takes the place of the distortion usually found in other dreams. In other words the dream represents a repressed wish to sleep with his mother and the converted libido is masked behind the fear for the father. His father was furious whenever he found him sleeping with his mother and our patient dreaded lest he should be detected by his father. The dream repeats the same state of mind and thus gives us the key to his neurosis. By sleeping with his mother to so late an age the incestuous feelings were kept alive and fixed on her, but as he grew older he energetically defended himself against them and finally succeeded in repressing them from consciousness. As a reaction to these unconscious desires he became extremely moral and religious and avoided anything sexual. At the age of twenty-eight he attempted coitus for the first time and failed. This failure was repeated at every subsequent attempt. He could not accomplish the sexual act because of the sexual fixation on the mother. Every woman unconsciously recalled his mother and, because of the marked repression of his incestuous feelings, coitus was naturally impossible. This was also constellated by his unconscious fear of his father. The patient was cured of his impotence as soon as these mechanisms were laid bare and explained to him.

Conscious incestuous feelings and experiences in adult life are not as rare as one would imagine. This subject has been discussed by Krafft-Ebing, Bloch, Havelock Ellis and others. My own observations in this regard taught me that sexual feelings and fancies about one's parents, sisters and brothers are not only extremely common in early life in the form of fancies and speculations about sex, but that they also often exist later. Nor must it be imagined that whenever it is found we deal with defective persons. The individual circumstances must always be considered, it is well known to those who investigate the psychosexual development that the sexual fancies indulged in by the individual at the pubescent period invariably refer to the parent. Havelock Ellis[12] explains the abhorrence of incest on the basis of familiarity. He states that "The normal failure of the pairing instinct to manifest itself in the case of brothers and sisters or of boys and girls brought up together from infancy is a merely negative phenomenon due to the inevitable absence under those circumstances of the conditions which evoke the pairing impulse" (p. 205). "Passion between brothers and sisters is, indeed, by no means so rare as is sometimes supposed, and it may be very strong, but it is usually aroused by the aid of those conditions which are normally required for the appearance of passion, more especially by the unfamiliarity caused by long separation" (p. 206). I agree with Havelock Ellis as far as he goes, but it seems to me that unfamiliarity plays only a subordinate part in the promotion of certain feelings between brothers and sisters. Unfamiliarity does not necessarily cause attraction between strangers of the opposite sexes, but long separation, especially when occurring since early life, is sure to produce a strong fascination between brothers and sisters. This is due to the repressed Oedipus complex. As was said above, every woman that later comes into the individual's life is unconsciously compared to the mother image in our unconscious. It is quite obvious that the sister fits into this image much better than any other woman. Who resembles the mother more than the daughter? Besides, the daughter has the advantage over the mother of youth and beauty. In this connection I would like to give an incident related to me by a colleague:

He came to this country from Germany at the age of fourteen years having left at home a sister one and a half years his junior. Years later he visited an exhibition in the Grand Central Palace in New York City and was strongly fascinated by a young lady he saw there. The attraction was so strong that he lost interest in the exhibits and followed her around until she left the place. Nor did this fascination end here. He told me that for months he acted like a man in love and for years he measured every woman by his "Grand Central Girl." He returned to his native city after having been eighteen years in America and as soon as he saw his younger sister the thought flashed through his mind, "Here is my Grand Central Girl." There was, indeed, a remarkable resemblance between his sister and the unknown young woman with whom he fell in love in America. His sister was the picture of his mother.

Moreover in real life, daughters often take the place of their mothers. I know of a few cases where men first loved the mothers and then switched over to the daughters. The daily press sometimes reports such cases.[13]

It is in the psychoses, however, that one sees the marked influence of the Oedipus complex. Here the complex usually comes to the surface in the form of symptoms, in hallucinations and delusions, and the analysis can generally trace these automatisms to early repressed feelings and experiences. The following cases will serve as paradigms:

CASE I.—V, twenty-nine years old, suffers from the paranoid form of dementia præcox. He hears voices accusing him of having had sexual relations with his mother. Analysis showed that as a boy he entertained sexual fancies about his mother. He often looked through the keyhole when she took her bath.

CASE II.—Mrs. F., a married woman of twenty-eight years, is a paranoid præcox. For more than a year she has been laughing and talking to herself uttering words like "clean, never, respectable, not at all, none." When questioned she states that she hears voices who accuse her of having been "too intimate with her father and brother" and the words uttered are only answers to her imaginary accusers. They read as follows: I am clean. I never did such terrible things. I am respectable. It is not at all true that I had sexual relations with my father and brother."

CASE III.—With Dr. H. Valentine Wildman I have recently committed a young man to the River Crest Sanatorium. This patient was paranoid and his main delusions were fairly well systematized. They were directed against his mother. He called her vile names and accused her of having made sexual advances to him. The following remarks pointing to a retrospective falsification contain the nucleus of his delusions: "I remember when I was a kid, she (mother) looked at my eyes and then paced the floor as if to say 'you are for me' and since then she wanted to make me her lover." The history of the case shows the typical mechanisms of paranoia, that is, there was fixation in narcism and mother love (he was the mother's favorite), defence against homosexual wish phantasies, then failure of repression, as manifested in some homosexual experiences and delusions of persecution.[14]

Now it may be asked whether children show by their behavior any indication of the Oedipus complex and whether fathers realize consciously that their sons are their rivals. Anamneses taken from normal and abnormal persons answer these questions in the affirmative. Also the works of Freud, Bleuler, Jung, Putnam, Ferenczi, Stekel, Abraham, Rank, Jones,[15] and others, show beyond any doubt that this is the case. To quote Bleuler, "After our attention had been called to it we found this Oedipus complex more and more frequently. It is also an important factor in the selection of lovers among normal and abnormal persons."[16] I have collected many, many facts. Some I have personally observed and some were given to me by reliable colleagues and friends, showing that beyond any doubt small children often wish to replace the parent of their own sex. A mother told me that her bright and healthy little boy of two years is very jealous of his father, and shows it on every occasion. Seeing her talking and sitting next to her husband he ran to her and pulled her away, exclaiming, "No Mami talk Daddy, sit down talk Baby." A brilliant little boy of three years, hearing that he will sleep with his mother because his father was going to stay away for the night, expressed his great pleasure to his mother, and added, "Let us play that we are married. I'll call you Mary and you call me John" (names of parents). Later, when he entered his mother's sleeping room, he said, "Here comes your husband." A little girl of three and one-half years on being punished by her mother exclaimed in her childish way, "Go away to Susie (her dead sister), I can be papa's Mama (meaning his wife, as her father calls her mother 'mama')." Another little girl of about four years kissed her father and kept on repeating, "I love you so much, papa. Let's go to the Bronx and never come home to mama." And on being questioned she admitted that she did not love her mother.

Some parents directly encourage incestuous love by sleeping with their children until a late age and thus stimulate them prematurely. This is done through ignorance but unconsciously because it furnishes an outlet to the parent. A striking example of this kind is the following: A psychopathic mother consulted me about her eleven years old boy "because of late he acted almost like a man" when sleeping with her. Investigation showed that this boy had slept with his mother most of the time because his father, a traveling salesman, was away from home from four to six months at a time. The mother stated that she was afraid to sleep alone, and in spite of her observations, which lead her to consult me, she refused to give up this pleasure. When I tried to impress her that the boy was at the pubescent age and that such actions must be expected if he slept with her or with any other woman she accused me of being an alarmist.

It is not uncommon for parents to be jealous of the love shown by the other parent for the child. A glaring example of this kind was reported to me by a patient referred to me by Dr. Coriat of Boston. Her husband was a very prominent business man, but somewhat eccentric. She was very much attached to her only son and the more she loved him the more he was hated by the father. The latter openly expressed his jealousy and hatred for his son and treated him most cruelly whenever he could do so. This feeling continued for more than thirty years until the father died, and was the cause of much unhappiness.

In his study on incest among savages[17] Freud showed that the incest shyness is an infantile trait and in striking accord with the psychic life of the neurotic. Psychoanalysis teaches that the first sexual object of the boy is of an incestuous prohibitive nature directed against the mother or sister; it also shows us how the developing individual frees himself from these feelings. The neurotic individual, however, regularly presents a fragment of psychic infantilism. He is either unable to free himself from the infantile relations of psychosexuality, or he has returned to them. It is for that reason that the incestuous fixations of the libido continue to play a great part in his unconscious psychic life.

REFERENCES

1. Sammlung kleine Schriften zur Neurosenlehre, Zweite Folge.
2. Freud: The Interpretation of Dreams. The Macmillan Co., New York, and George Allen Co., London.
3. Freud: *L. c.*, p. 221.
4. *L. c.*, p. 223.
5. Act IV, Sc. 3, translated by Clark.
6. Freud: *L. c.*, p. 246.
7. Freud: *L. c.*, p. 246. On Stairway Dreams.
8. *Cf.* Chap. XIV.
9. For the mechanism of such traumas see Freud: Selected papers on Hysteria, p. 159.
10. *Cf.* Chap. XIV.
11. Ferenczi: Analytische Deutung und Behandlung der psychosexuellen Impotenz beim Manne. Psychiatrisch-neurologische Wochenschrift, 1908, No. 35. See also the works of Stekel, and Steiner: Die Psychischen Störungen der Männlichen Potenz. Deuticke, Wien.
12. Sexual Selection in Man, p. 204.

13. Those who are interested in the problem may read an excellent paper on the subject by Freud: Die Inzestscheu der Wilden; Imago, Heft 1. Also Totem und Taboo (translated by A. A. Brill, Moffat Yard & Co., New York), 1918.

14. For full particulars of these mechanisms, see Chap. X.

15. See especially, "The Oedpius Complex as an Explanation of Hamlet's Mystery," Amer. Jour. of Psychology, Jan., 1910.

16. Dementia Præcox oder Gruppe der Schizophrenien, p.344 . Deuticke, Leipzig u. Wien, 1911. Also his Manual of Psychiatry, a translation of which is in preparation.

17. Freud: *L. c.*

The Œdipus Hypothesis as a Psychological Measuring Unit. Its Evolution and Final Stabilization as a Social Force

It has been my experience to be frequently asked by physicians, "What do you mean by the Œdipus Complex?" For a long time I was unable to answer the question, largely because it was asked in jest, but further by reason of the fact that it was impossible for me to phrase a reply in a way which I felt would be satisfactory to my questioner. When asked partly in jest I would frequently reply, "What is the Ehrlich side-chain theory?" This is an apparent evasion. To others I have said, "It is a mode of explaining why any individual finds it difficult to break away from old ways of doing things in order to acquire new and better ones." Again to others, my reply has been, "It is a restatement of the world-old struggle of conservatism versus progressivism." Such a method of handling what Freud has termed the "root-complex" of the neurosis will hardly suffice. Yet after all the answers just enumerated may be found satisfactory if elaborated.

In the first place the Œdipus Complex is solely an hypothesis, just as the Ehrlich side-chain theory is an hypothesis. It is a formulation to be used to handle the facts. Instead of terming it only the "root-complex" of the neurosis, however, I purpose giving it a much broader basis. It can be used as a unit of measurement for all psychological situations, not only for those "variations which are only perceived when they become great or inconvenient," and hence called abnormal, but for every so-called normal psychical activity as well. Even the tyro in science knows that the idea "normal" is a pure bugaboo. Normal means average if it means anything.

Just as we use a foot-rule to measure all space relations; a unit of time for all time relations, so the Œdipus hypothesis can be used as a unit for the comprehending of psychical situations. It is the only unit which has proved itself valid for all psychical phenomena, be they what intellectualists call normal or abnormal.

I think I may say that practically every philosophical hypothesis, save pragmatism, has neglected what are called pathological data, overlooking the fact that pathological does not mean of a different, qualitative, nature, but simply a variant which must be measured by the same standards as that which is called normal.

In this connection one may again turn to that ancient sophist Protagoras for the first statement of a sound pragmatism. In his dialogue with Morosophus on the perception of truth, Protagoras closes an eloquent peroration with the question: "Do you know Xanthias the son of Glaucus?"

Morosophus: Yes, but he seemed to me a very *ordinary* man and quite unfit to aid in such inquiries.

Protagoras: To me he seemed quite wonderful and a great proof of the truth I have maintained. For the wretch was actually unable to distinguish red from green, the color of the grass from that of blood! You may imagine how he dressed, and how his taste was derided. But it was his eye, and not his taste, that was at fault. I questioned him closely and am sure he could not help it. He simply saw colors differently. How and why I was not able to make out. But it was from his case and others like it, but less startling, that I learned that truth and reality are to each man what appears to him. For the differences, I am sure, exist, even though they are not noticed unless they are very great and inconvenient.

Morosophus: But surely Xanthias was diseased, and his judgments about colors are of no more importance than those of a madman.

Protagoras: You do not get rid of the difficulty by calling it madness and disease. And how would you define the essential nature of madness and disease?

Morosophus: I am sure I do not know. You should ask Asklepios.

To which Protagoras remarks: "Ah! he is one of those gods I have never been able to meet."

One does not get rid of difficulties by calling them abnormal. Giving them this appellation does not explain them. Hence the Œdipus hypothesis may be utilized to analyze everybody's activities, not those of the neurotic alone. To say that only the neurotic has to deal with an Œdipus fantasy is absurd; everybody does: but how? The way the individual handles his Œdipus fantasy; how far it has evolved away from its infantile stages, this is what determines whether he shall be termed neurotic or not, normal or abnormal.

What then is the Œdipus hypothesis? For the sake of historical completeness it may be recalled that it received its name from the drama of Œdipus Rex, a mythological theme in great favor among the Greeks of the Epic period. The psychoanalyst should read the various renderings of it. It is fully treated psychoanalytically in "The Myth of the Birth of the Hero"[1] by Rank, also in the same author's "Inzest Motive," both of which works have been mentioned.

To the philistine the story simply means that Œdipus killed his father and married his mother; but it implies infinitely more than this. It is the psychical elaboration of an enormously important part of a biological instinct. It is the conversion of energy into symbolic activities that at lower social stages was expended at physical levels.

How this evolution towards the conversion of energy into symbolic form took place cannot be entered into fully here.

Freud has shown in his "Three Contributions to the Theory of Sex"[2] that on rigid analysis the instinct of reproduction reduces itself to the choice of a proper *object*—the object choice; and of the proper *aim,* i. e., the reproductive act. To satisfy the first requirement an individual of the opposite sex must be the libido object. This sounds so trite as to hardly require stating, yet the merest superficial acquaintance with human as well as infrahuman activities reveals how much variation of attraction exists in a direction away from the consciously obvious heterosexual object.

The second requirement is successfully met with when the partial libido trends already discussed on page 40, become united to successfully establish the primacy of the genital zone. The variations from this equally obvious goal are also so frequent that the observant inquirer is struck with amazement at the various faulty adjustments of what is so frequently considered a "natural" function.

We are now speaking solely of mechanisms which have been laid down for many million years and which are instinctively and unconsciously forming, but, it must be recalled, they are extremely variable in their external modifications when it comes

[1] Monograph Series, No. 18.
[2] Second English edition from third German edition, 1916.

to their permitted socially-controlled and consciously-guided activities.

It is to this broad reproductive instinct, in all of its conscious and unconscious manifestations, that Freud has applied the term sexual. In this present volume on the Technique of Psychoanalysis, *sexual* means any human contact actual or symbolic by means of any sensory area with the object of the same or of the opposite sex, which has *productive creation* for its *purpose*, be it concretely in the form of a child, or symbolically as an invention, artistic production, or other type of mutually creative product. It does not apply to those contacts which have purely nutritive or self-preservation instinct behind it. And it does not apply solely to genital contacts.

Thus it might be stated, though such a statement might seem to be paradoxical, that prostitution is not really sexual. It has come to be stigmatized because it utilizes the love principle for purposes of gain, and stands as a symbol of the destruction of society rather than that of its upbuilding. If in biblical phrases, "the love of money is the root of all evil" then prostitution symbolizes that root, and as later will be pointed out it represents in its pure type chiefly an infantile anal erotic complex. It is a satisfaction of unconscious hate rather than of love in terms of the Œdipus hypothesis.

The Œdipus hypothesis then attempts to establish some criterion, or group of criteria, by which human conduct may be valued as it looks forward to ultimate social or pragmatic truth, or goodness. It first directs attention to the biological trend of getting away from the type represented by the parent of the same sex, to a getting toward the type represented by the parent of the opposite sex. Without this biological direction of libido, no concrete social structure is possible. It is not father hate and mother love for the boy, and vice versa for the girl, in terms of conscious psychology, as is so often said by the critics. The Œdipus hypothesis has nothing whatever to do with conscious psychology, any more than the chemical formulæ of the fats in butter have to do with milking a cow. A knowledge of these formulæ for fats may prove the ultimate basis for the valuation of a herd of cows, just as the application of the Œdipus formulæ will permit of the comprehension of the acts of a family and thus determine their social value.

So-called shrewd practical observers may make excellent estimates of cows as well as of citizens, but when it comes to correcting the mistakes, in order to get shrewder and more practical observations, some measuring instruments are needed. Hence psychoanalysis utilizes the Œdipus instrument of precision.

In obtaining the full family history the analyst is getting the material from which a proper estimate of the evolution of the patient's psyche may be gathered. This it must be remembered is the conscious estimate of the patient's relations to the members of his family.

These conscious attitudes to the members of the family group are not, however, invariable criteria of his more fundamental unconscious ones, yet they are of great importance in affording clues to early infantile repressions. The family is the first training camp, as it were, for the child's activities in gaining his social bearings. His later attitude toward men, women and things is patterned largely after his infantile models. We can here trace the workings of the Œdipus formula in its gradual evolution away from phantasy to reality.

This formula has shown that the boy must have certain attitudes toward others of the same sex, mostly antagonisms, from the primitive wellspring of energy, and attractions toward all others of an opposite sex.

A young woman to whom, in the early days of my psychoanalytic work, I had announced the Œdipus principle rather crudely, responded with much heat, "But I have always loved my mother, and we three sisters are devotedly attached to one another. The idea of rivalry among us sisters is impossible."

"Yes, yes," I said, "that is true, but you are speaking of your conscious attitudes. We will not comprehend the pain between your shoulder blades by accepting the conscious attitude as the whole story, we must see what is on the other side of the picture."

It did not take long, by the study of the unconscious processes, to find that the pain between the shoulder blades was the symbol of a "stab in the back" from her, consciously, most loved sister. Behind it lay concealed a very intense rivalry, a rivalry which, as will be seen, is a necessary part of the working out of the Œdipus idea, and one which, it may be maintained, is a necessary aspect of a comprehensive biological scheme for social evolution. The sister was really trying to steal her sweetheart. She was " stabbing her in the back."

This biological scheme has been stressed particularly by Rank in his study on the " Myth of the Birth of the Hero " and he has called it the "family neurotic romance."[8] It is a universal phenomenon, and must be worked out with each patient. They must see for themselves how they have evolved their own dream of power in opposition to all the other members of the family.

I am assuming that Rank's fundamental study will be read by one interested in mastering the technique of psychoanalysis, yet it belongs in this place in the development of the Œdipus hypothesis and a short résumé of the chief principles involved is desirable.

Every child is an egoist. It has been seen why this must be so in order that he may live at all. It is equally obvious that if social adaptation is to take place, he cannot remain one, at least not at an infantile level. Every child, in his egocentric fashion, constructs for himself therefore his little hero-myth. The will for power, in danger, thrusts in a phantasy substitute and thus aids the work of repression, as we have already discussed. Inasmuch as the stages through which any one individual child may go are usually much abbreviated, and difficult of interpretation by himself, of himself most of all—that is why most of us deny we have ever had such fancies—Rank turned to a study of the hero myths of the world, and by a comparative study of these ancient sagas, was able to reconstruct what goes on in every child probably, although, for many, such processes are hidden. The evolutionary principle of recapitulation again does service in the understanding of these psychical structures.

The standard principle for these ancient hero-myths is formulated as follows: " The hero is the child of most distinguished parents; usually the son of a king (with us some important personage, governor, millionaire, or what not). His origin is preceded by difficulties, such as continence, or prolonged barrenness, or secret union of the parents, due to external prohibitions or obstacles. During the pregnancy, or antedating the same, there is a prophecy, in form of a dream, or an oracle, cautioning against his birth, and usually threatening danger to the father or to his representative. As a rule he is surrendered to the water, in a box. He is then saved by animals, or by lowly people (shep-

[8] Monograph Series, No. 18.

herds), and is suckled by a female animal, or by a humble woman. After he has grown up he finds his distinguished parents, in a highly versatile manner, takes his revenge upon his father, on the one hand, is acknowledged on the other, and finally achieves rank and honors."

This is the child phantasy of the race, in highly condensed form. Even in the mythological stories themselves, this ground pattern, as it were, is departed from, and it is therefore conceivable that one rarely finds it in pure form at the present time, save in some psychotics, particularly in the group which, as defined by Bleuler and Jung, is termed schizophrenia, or dementia præcox. Here the ancient formula is repeated true to type. In minor degrees and in the greatest variety of disguises the psychoneurotic follows out parts of the program. As Freud has pointed out these individuals remain children or infantile in certain aspects of their strivings; they are close to the unconscious. As Rank has put it, "The fancies of neurotics are, as it were, the uniformly exaggerated reproductions of the childish imaginings." But as we have so often remarked, these are closed to the ordinary modes of investigation and the psychoanalytic method has become the best method of reaching them at the present time.

Rank has sketched the chief outlines of the biological need for getting away from the parents. "Except ye leave father and mother, ye shall not enter the kingdom of heaven," I conceive to be a much earlier statement of the same situation. In the realm of plant life Darwin's penetrating studies that showed the values of cross-fertilization is collateral evidence in a realm of biological activities far below man, and the whole biological scheme of things reveals the ceaseless experiments that nature goes through with in the hope that advanced types may result. Just what particular evolutionary formula will appeal to the analyst or analyzed, should one be invoked at all, whether it smacks of Neodarwinism, Neolamarckianism, or follows out the Mendelian principle, or De Vries's Mutation hypothesis, not to mention others, is absolutely immaterial in the development of the general idea. If the patient should be an out and out opponent to any evolutionary hypothesis at all, then the whole psychoanalytic scheme will have little value to him. In general, I assume that the analyst has a working knowledge of the general biological hypotheses concerning evolution and heredity.

In the human family, psychoanalysis emphasizes, as Rank

has phrased it, "the detachment of the growing individual from the authority of the parents is one of the most necessary, but also one of the most painful achievements of evolution. It is absolutely necessary for this detachment to take place." Analysis shows how the psychoneurotic is endeavoring to accomplish the task and also indicates how the healthier individual has really accomplished it in various ways. The manner of cure, or the rationale of psychoanalysis, how it acts, may be very definitely demonstrated in the tracing of the individual's growing independence from his parental complexes.

To still further illustrate this absolutely essential separation I not infrequently use a simple illustration. Putting the problem of the apple tree, I ask, "What would happen if all the seeds should attempt to grow under the parent tree?" It is an easy step from this illustration to a discussion of the thousands of devices which plants and animals have elaborated to make sure of the dispersal of their seeds or offspring. The ingenious clinging seeds that fasten to one's clothes or to the fur of animals, the various winged seeds that fly like the thistledown, or dandelion, those that float, or those that pass through the intestines of animals, the devices are legion and the ingenuity marvellous.[4] Parent and child must be separated.

"Social progress—speaking now of higher forms—is essentially based upon this opposition of the two generations," writes Rank, who then points out how the failure to get away from the parent is paramount to a neurosis.

"For the young child, the parents are in the first place the sole authority, and the source of all faith. To resemble them, *i. e.*, the progenitor of the same sex; to grow up like father or mother, this is the most intense and portentous wish of the child's early years. Progressive intellectual development naturally brings it about that the child gradually becomes acquainted with the category to which the parents belong. Other parents become known to the child, who compares these with his own, and thereby becomes justified in doubting the incomparability and uniqueness with which he had invested them. Trifling occurrences in the life of the child, which induce a mood of dissatisfaction, lead up to a criticism of the parents, and the gathering conviction that other parents are preferable in certain ways, is utilized for this

[4] Consult Koerner von Marilaun, Natural History of Plants; Fabre, Souvenirs Entomologiques.

attitude of the child toward the parents. From the psychology of the neuroses, we have learned that very intense emotions of sexual rivalry are also involved in this connection. The causative factor evidently is the feeling of being neglected. Opportunities arise only too frequently when the child is neglected, or at least feels himself negected, when he misses the entire love of the parents, or at least regrets having to share the same with the other children of the family. The feeling that one's own inclinations are not entirely reciprocated seeks its relief in the idea—often consciously remembered from very early years—of being a stepchild, or an adopted child. Many persons who have not become neurotics, very frequently remember occasions of this kind, when the hostile behavior of parents was interpreted and reciprocated by them in this fashion, usually under the influence of story books. The influence of sex is already evident, in so far as the boy shows a far greater tendency to harbor hostile feelings against his father than his mother, with a much stronger inclination to emancipate himself from the father than from the mother. The imaginative faculty of girls is possibly much less active in this respect. These consciously remembered psychic emotions of the years of childhood supply the factor which permits the interpretation of the myth. What is not often consciously remembered, but can almost invariably be demonstrated through psychoanalysis, is the next stage in the development of this incipient alienation from the parents, which may be designated by the term *Family Romance of Neurotics*. The essence of neurosis, and of all higher mental qualifications, comprises a special activity of the imagination which is primarily manifested in the play of the child, and which from about the period preceding puberty takes hold of the theme of the family relations. A characteristic example of this special imaginative faculty is represented by the familiar day dreams, which are continued until long after puberty. Accurate observation of these day dreams shows that they serve for fulfilment of wishes, for the righting of life, and that they have two essential objects, one erotic, the other of an ambitious nature (usually with the erotic factor concealed therein). About the time in question the child's imagination is engaged upon the task of getting rid of the parents, who are now despised and are as a rule to be supplanted by others of a higher social rank. The child utilizes an accidental coincidence of actual happenings (meetings with the lord of the

28

manor, or the proprietor of the estate, in the country; with the reigning prince, in the city; in the United States with some great statesman, millionaire). Accidental occurrences of this kind arouse the child's envy, and this finds its expression in fancy fabrics[5] which replace the two parents by others of a higher rank. The technical elaboration of these two imaginings, which, of course, by this time have become conscious, depends upon the child's adroitness, and also upon the material at his disposal. It likewise enters into consideration, if these fancies are elaborated with more or less claim to plausibility. This stage is reached at a time when the child is still lacking all knowledge of the sexual conditions of descent. With the added knowledge of the manifold sexual relations of father and mother; with the child's realization of the fact that the father is always uncertain, whereas the mother is very certain—the family romance undergoes a peculiar restriction; it is satisfied with ennobling the father, while the descent from the mother is no longer questioned, but accepted as an unalterable fact. The second (or sexual) stage of the family romance is moreover supported by another motive, which did not exist in the first or asexual stage. Knowledge of sexual matters gives rise to the tendency of picturing erotic situations and relations, impelled by the pleasurable emotion of placing the mother, or the subject of the greatest sexual curiosity, in the situation of secret unfaithfulness and clandestine love affairs. In this way the primary or asexual fantasies are raised to the standard of the improved later understanding.

"The motive of revenge and retaliation, which was originally in the front, is again evident. These neurotic children are mostly those who were punished by the parents, to break them of bad sexual habits, and they take their revenge upon their parents by their imaginings. The younger children of a family are particularly inclined to deprive their predecessors of their advantage by fables of this kind (exactly as in the intrigues of history). Frequently they do not hesitate in crediting the mother with as many love affairs as there are rivals. An interesting variation of this family romance restores the legitimacy of the plotting hero himself, while the other children are disposed

[5] Compare Freud, Hysterical Fancies, and Their Relation to Bisexuality, with references to the literature on this subject. This contribution is contained in the second series of the Collection of Short Articles on the Neurosis Doctrine, Vienna and Leipsig, 1909.

of in this way as illegitimate. The family romance may be governed besides by a special interest, all sorts of inclinations being met by its adaptability and variegated character. The little romancer gets rid in this fashion, for example, of the kinship of a sister, who may have attracted him sexually.

"Those who turn aside with horror from this corruption of the child mind, or perhaps actually contest the possibility of such matters, should note that all these apparently hostile imaginings have not such a very bad significance after all, and that the original affection of the child for his parents is still preserved under their thin disguise. The faithlessness and ingratitude on the part of the child are only apparent, for on investigating in detail the most common of these romantic fancies, namely the substitution of both parents, or of the father alone, by more exalted personages—the discovery will be made that these new and highborn parents are invested throughout with the qualities which are derived from real memories of the true lowly parents, so that the child does not actually remove his father but exalts him. *The entire endeavor to replace the real father by a more distinguished one is merely the expression of the child's longing for the vanished happy time, when his father still appeared to be the strongest and greatest man, and the mother seemed the dearest and most beautiful woman.*

"The child turns away from the father, as he now knows him, to the father in whom he believed in his earlier years, his imagination being in truth only the expression of regret for this happy time having passed away. Thus the over-valuation of the earliest years of childhood again claims its own in these fancies.⁶ An interesting contribution to this subject is furnished by the study of the dreams. Dream interpretation teaches that even in later years, in the dreams of the emperor or the empress, these princely persons stand for the father and mother. Thus the infantile over-valuation of the parents is still preserved in the dream of the normal adult.

"As we proceed to fit the preceding features into our scheme, we feel justified in analogizing the ego of the child with the hero of the myth, in view of the unanimous tendency of family romances and hero myths; keeping in mind that the myth throughout reveals an endeavor to get rid of the parents, and that the same wish arises in the phantasies of the individual child at the time when it is trying to establish its personal independence.

The ego in the child behaves in this respect like the hero of the myth, and as a matter of fact, the hero should always be interpreted merely as a collective ego, which is equipped with all the excellences. In a similar manner, the hero in personal poetic fiction usually represents the poet himself, or at least one side of his character."

The beginner who, for the first time, approaches these mechanisms of getting away from the parents, has really only the faintest conception how the scheme works in everyday life. I must reiterate to him that he constantly keep in mind all of the partial libido trends. Each must be followed out in its most minute series of transformations, and the patient gradually sees for himself, in some special form of conduct, such as love for certain forms of play, nutrition customs, likes and dislikes of all kinds, just how successful or not his getting away from his infantile attachments has been. Every infantile attachment means locked-up energy, which cannot be used for useful work. They are the "messengers from the unconscious," which Bergson speaks of, "which escaping through the half open door, remind us of what we are dragging behind us unawares."

I wish to illustrate these points by a partial statement of an actual history and by means of a diagram:

This patient was a young man of 28 years of age, of good family. His father was a successful business man. He had two brothers, older than himself, and two sisters living; one sister had died. He began to drink at sixteen, smoked since he was ten. His father was a drinking man, at times excessively so, also one brother. He went through school and entered college but did not persist, as his gradually increased drinking bouts interrupted the discipline, of which there was little at home. He went into business but did not apply himself particularly. He was a charming, good-looking, " gentleman's " son with plenty of money.

His drinking bouts were becoming more or less continuous. He would be feeling perfectly well, would take a drink, usually of whiskey, then another, and from that time nothing short of a strait-jacket could hold him; he was suave and courteous and convincing if he had his own way, but he would be a very rough

⁶ For the idealizing of the parents by the children, compare Maeder's comments (*Jahr. f. Psychoanalyse*, p. 152, and *Centralblatt f. Psychoanalyse*, I, p. 51), on Varendonk's essay, Les idéals d'enfant, Tome VII, 1908.

customer if opposed. After twelve, twenty-four, thirty-six or sometimes seventy-two hours or more of this he would be a wreck and would have to be taken care of. Sometimes the bout would last two or three weeks. They were becoming frequent, and his last bout, before I saw him, was attended with meningeal symptoms and signs of general toxemia, mild jaundice, etc.

The picture is familiar to many. I do not intend to detail the analysis, I shall only utilize some of the facts revealed to show, in part, what the whole thing meant, in terms of the working out of the Œdipus hypothesis, the family neurotic romance, and the later phase of this same situation, namely narcissism.

Analysis uncovered a great deal of material, but I wish only to direct attention to this patient's eating habits by way of illustrating the meaning of what this chapter seeks to emphasize, namely the failure to develop away from the infantile manner of handling the Œdipus phantasy.

Asking him one day what he ate for breakfast he said, "Sausages, waffles and maple syrup," and for supper? "I don't remember."

And yesterday for breakfast? "Sausages, waffles and maple syrup." He could not remember what else he had eaten. Every morning he ate the same breakfast, and had done so for fifteen years or more. He ate no vegetables, except potatoes; he ate a variety of meats.

Now what has this to do with the Œdipus hypothesis?

Before we go further with the discussion let me put in a diagrammatic form what is the general scheme I am after. I shall again utilize the diagram (modified in circular form) that has already been used to show the first steps in libido distribution following birth.[7] It is not meant to show every detail in the evolution of the partial libido trends—it is, as was the preceding diagram, only suggestive.

All of our present-day activities, which manifest themselves in the various life contacts, may for our purpose be represented by a circle. At the periphery we may arrange the conscious acts of daily life. In this diagram the libido area distributions are arbitrarily represented by six sectors, showing the first distributions, *i. e.*, the partial libido trends, already discussed (see p. 40). I have only partially elaborated one sector, *i. e.*, the nutritive sector, since I am engaged in placing the dietary habits of the

[7] Page 40.

patient under discussion somewhere in the scheme. If the discussion should have turned on why a patient ended his sentences in a little giggle, or another toyed with a button on his coat most of the time, the particular evolution might have been shown in

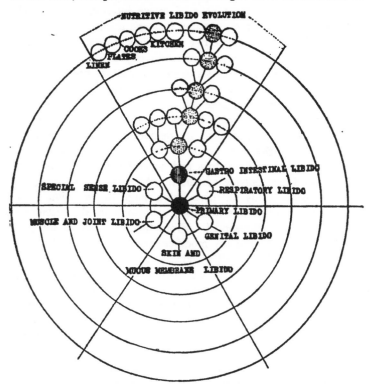

Diagrammatic suggestion of the evolution of the libido trends. The path taken by the patient's nutritive interests, and hence his sympathetic contacts (social evolution particularly of his sociability) have become narrowed to a persistent restricted and narrow diet, the meaning for which, in his individual case, meant failure to get away from the parents, i. e., in the unconscious sense of the Œdipus formula. The diagram suggests the line taken by this in the slightly shaded circles.

the respiratory, or the skin sectors, which for the purposes of this illustration are here left blank. I am engaged in placing this particular patient's partial libido trends, as far as one particular series of acts are concerned, in relation to the Œdipus concept.

This boy's first nutritive libido concerned itself with his mother's breast. Milk was his sole food. This is diagrammatically shown on the first circle, in which the initial partial libido trends are represented. From here on, it may be inferred, the evolution of man's nutritive interests becomes more and more complex, until at the stage of evolved manhood, the nutritive libido occupies a large part of man's interests. In the U. S. Census for 1900, it is estimated that one third of the adult population of the U. S., some twenty million at least, make their living in pursuits which contribute directly to the nutritive libido. Here we see man's interests, into which active energy goes, concerning itself with pots and pans, agricultural instruments, crops, etc. I need not complete the picture. It is so obvious. Yet when we come to discuss the patient's nutritive libido we find a very striking fact, that of its monotony. It has not evolved. He has eaten the same breakfast for the past sixteen years, eats no vegetables save potatoes and several meats. He has no interest in foods outside of this limited dietary. If I should attempt to place his nutritive libido stage of evolution I would place it at an infantile level, say arbitrarily on the second circle, which is here represented. From this point on to the present it has not undergone any modification, as has been schematically shown. I might say all sociability, so far as these nutritive interests are concerned, is thus restricted.

Now, turning to the mother-father relationships, the first fact that strikes one is its failure to branch out. It remains closer to a monotonous infantile food—milk—and fails to show a wider, richer dietary. I am not generalizing about the significance of a limited dietary for all people. Every tub stands on its own bottom. Here I am simply taking a particular case and seeing what it means for this particular individual. It represents, in terms of the Œdipus concept, an infantile attachment to the mother. It is a way by which he unconsciously and symbolically hangs on to the mother. Let me now add that milk is also taken instead of coffee, tea or cocoa. Free associations, with milk, concerning which we shall speak, brings the patient directly to his mother. Interesting also free associations on sausages show that he prefers small ones, thin ones, and mother's "nipple" turns up in his associations, as well as the word "penis."

Associations to "waffles," also, brings us to "nipples," "teats," to the "irons in which they are cooked"—"colored woman's breasts," "pigs' tits," were some of the free associations.

I shall not give further details to show unconscious associations establishing the relationships between the infantile mother phantasy and the dietary customs making up this monotonous breakfast.

We have seen, however, that the Œdipus hypothesis involves two contrasting situations, one of unconscious attachment to the parent image of the opposite sex, the other connoted by the unconscious antagonism to the father-brother image. There is plenty of evidence to show the unconscious desire to get rid of his father and brother in his drinking bouts. It is further extremely valuable to note that this diet also represents a "castration motive," meaning symbolically the overcoming of the father. Furthermore, the only other feature of his diet, namely his free choice of meats, has an intricate motivation. For him, as for many children, meats and vegetables fall into the strong and weak group respectively. Animism so regards them, and the young human passes through this psychological animistic phase. Many people, as we know, never get away from their crude animistic notions regarding foods, and a study of these makes many dietary faddisms comprehensible and fascinating. Meats are to make him strong and powerful. They therefore will help him in overcoming his father, or his representative, his older brother.

I have very rapidly sketched some of the salient points in the elucidation of the food habits of this patient and wish to stress more particularly their failure to evolve and therefore the gap in this individual's interests which is the center of endeavor for 25 per cent. of all of the people he meets. I might say for purposes of illustration, that he thus cuts himself out of sympathetic contact and interest from one quarter of his entire social environment by this simple failure of development—by this unconscious utilization of the Œdipus fantasy as seen in his dietary customs. He limits thereby a very important factor in the freeing himself from the limited family group to enter the larger social groups, namely the factor of sociability as it is termed.

I need not go on to say that a similar failure to develop along a number of other libido channels has contracted his sympathetic social contacts, i. e., his sociability, down to a minimum. This is a part of the motivation for his drinking. It aids him to get away from the consciousness of his inferiority. But I only started out to give a concrete example of how the Œdipus hypothesis is applicable to a specific bit of conduct.

I shall only add that every bit of conduct, every taste, or inclination, like or dislike, is capable of a similar analysis, and the analytic technique aids the patient to see how his everyday acts have come to have the value and significance that they have.

When the subject of the utilization of the dream is taken up we shall see that the evidence is overwhelming with reference to the constant activity of the Œdipus phantasy.

We then return to the point from which we started, that the Œdipus hypothesis is utilized as a sort of measuring rod to determine the grade of evolution of psychological activities, looking forward to ultimate social values. The analysis of one's acts shows, schematically speaking, how far on the circles of evolution the particular act may be placed, whether it remains an infantile fantasy way of obtaining satisfaction from the mother-father attachment or rejection (according to sex) or a grown up sublimation way which is socially, and hence also individually valuable. Identically the same energy is utilized, but "by their fruits shall ye know them."

OEDIPUS AND CASTRATION COMPLEXES

THE OEDIPUS COMPLEX

Using the terms Oedipus Complex, Parental Complex, and Family Romance, Freud and other psychoanalysts greatly emphasize an unconscious development of desire and a conflict concerning it which they insist arises in the unconscious phantasy life of a child during an early stage (the phallic stage) of development. The essence of the Oedipus Complex is libidinal striving taking the form of unconscious desire for sexual satisfaction with the parent of the opposite sex.

In this connection it must be remembered that whole dramas and conflicts can be developed and lived out in unconscious phantasies and can be handled by the unconscious Ego. To the Super-ego a phantasy, unconscious or conscious, has all the significance of an act and is thus capable of arousing a sense of guilt and a fear of punishment in the unconscious Ego. The immediate significance of this is that the Oedipus Complex, and the Castration Complex which is directly connected with it, may exist entirely in the Ucs and be coped with completely without ever entering consciousness. In other words, it is not the actual relationship to the parents which is dynamic, but rather a phenomenon arising spontaneously in the unconscious instinctual phantasy life.

The term, Oedipus complex, has been adopted from the Greek myth, concerning the life and fate of Oedipus which was the subject of tragedies by Sophocles and other Greek dramatists. But really, the original story does not at all fit the Oedipus situation as developed in the theory of the psychoanalysts. Oedipus, deserted in infancy by his parents and brought up by foster parents, meets his own father on the road and kills him without any knowledge that he was his own father and long before a later love relationship developed between Oedipus and his own mother. Also this love grew as between strangers, neither mother nor son realizing their relationship. But the whole chain of events was predicted and follows the line of "fate," so often dwelled on in Greek drama.

Earlier psychoanalysts used the term Electra complex when referring to the girl-father love-relationship, again taking over a term from a Greek myth. But this usage seems to have been discontinued and now the term Oedipus complex is employed for the love-relationships of children of both sexes with actual parents, parent-imagos, or other members of the family as they may become for the child a parent-surrogate.

The force of the Oedipus complex rests not only in its natural universal occurrence, but also in the usual taboo against incest among primitive as well as civilized people. Alexander says that the prohibition against incest remains active in the unconscious of the adult, and that this is the crux of the psychoanalytic theory, as is also the fact that the entire incest conflict later completely disappears from consciousness. He says, "The submergence of conscious moral inhibitions into the unconscious is a readily ascertainable fact."

Jones says of the Oedipus complex that it is "the most characteristic and important finding in all psychoanalysis, and against it is directed the whole strength of the individual's resistance as well as the external criticism of psychoanalysts. It is hardly an exaggeration to say that whatever manifold form this resistance may take, and whatever aspect of psychoanalysis is being criticized, it is the Oedipus that is finally responsible."

Thus the real basis of the parent complex is found not only in the universal parent-child situation and the experiences which are bound up with it as a result of infantile libidinal strivings, but it also has deeper roots in racial experiences which are carried over in the life of the young individual as inherited ideas. The theory of phylogenesis is thoroughly involved in the psychoanalytic notion of the development of the Oedipus Complex. Freud states that the unconscious psychic life of the child appears to recapitulate the evolution of the species. "In the soul-life of present-day children the same archaic moments still prevail which generally prevailed at the time of primitive civilization."

From their theory and from their analytic findings it comes about that immense stress has been laid by psychoanalysts on the Oedipus situation. They believe that evidences of the complex are to be discovered in every case analyzed, and contend that it is practically a universal experience. Indeed, it is believed to be a necessary stage in normal development; Freud calls it "a general human characteristic decreed by fate." He insists on the danger of underestimating rather than overestimating its importance in all personality development. Jones says, "All other conclusions of psycho-analytical theory are grouped around this complex, and by the truth of this finding psycho-analysis stands or falls."

The Oedipus Complex finds part of its conscious expression in the child's desire for various forms of physical intimacy with the parent, bodily contacts, caresses, sleeping with the parent, etc. On the unconscious side the libido is represented by a direct incest motive; the unconscious strivings are primitive in this respect, as in all others, and are for direct sexual satisfaction.

Out of this situation inevitably develops the sensing, both conscious and unconscious, of the parent of the same sex as standing in the way of desired gratification. Hostile impulses grow and are manifested more or less openly in such ways as expressions of joy at the parent's absence, the lack of wish for his or her return, the conscious phantasy or even openly expressed desire for sole possession of the parent. In the unconscious, the child is believed to

Freud contends that mythology and history, "the tangible record of the ideas which permeate the fancy of primitive man" support his phylogenetic theory of the Oedipus and Castration complexes.

Rank has shown how much of imaginative literature is constructed about the incest theme.

For Alexander the Oedipus complex is the most demanding of all traumatic situations. Its surmounting involves the twofold problem— first, the sublimation of the erotic relation to the mother, second, the transference of part of the freed libido on to the father, so the purely hostile attitude to him acquires an erotic component. After sublimation is effected, there will be simultaneous sublimated love for both parents and continued sublimation or distributions over a number of love-objects.

Alexander finds in Freud's recent instinct classification theories a new angle from which to approach the resolution of the Oedipus complex. He explains or reinterprets this phenomenon on the basis of instinct fusion and defusion, q. v. The aggressive impulses felt toward the parent of the same sex arise, he thinks, out of the death or destructive instinct, and their overcoming is by a process of fusion with the Eros or life instinct (erotization). He speaks also of the desirability of sublimating these destructive tendencies.

Alexander points out the danger of the aggressive feeling against the father being turned back on the self and becoming a self-destroying tendency of abnormal strength. The normal person, he says, has at his disposal outwardly directed destruction impulses which in the neurotic are directed against his own instinctual urges in the form of conscience inhibitions and need for punishment. Both symptoms and other self-punishment processes, he points out, permit the maintenance of Oedipus tendencies, combative as well as erotic.

have phantasies of killing or injuring (perhaps castrating) the rival parent and taking his or her place with the loved parent.

In the case of the *boy*, the Oedipus Complex in its simplest form arises from what is spoken of as an "anaclitic" origin. That is, a previously formed attachment to the mother as nurse, protector, etc. results naturally at the phallic stage in her becoming the love-object, now that impulses more specifically sexual begin to emerge. While this libidinal object-cathexis of the mother (or mother-imago) is evolving, another all-important element of the so-called Oedipus situation begins to emerge. The boy's primary identification with the father now becomes centered upon taking the father's place with the mother and thus the latter is felt to be an obstacle. The hostility, both conscious and unconscious, which then begins to arise toward him in this one respect results in ambivalence and conflict.

The Oedipus situation, however, is seldom as simple as stated above. Freud admits that it is very difficult to obtain a clear view of the facts in connection with the earliest object-choices and identifications and still more difficult to describe them intelligibly. This is due to "the complicating element introduced by bi-sexuality," constitutionally innate in all children. On the whole, he thinks it is always well to assume (at least in all cases of neuroses) the existence of what he calls the "complete Oedipus." By this he means that there will be present at the same time both a positive and a negative (or inverted) Oedipus situation; that is, the boy will combine (with various degrees of cathexis) a father identification and mother object-love with a mother identification and father object-love. The amount of cathexis distributed to either the positive or the negative situation depends partly upon the relative strength of the innate masculine or feminine disposition in the boy and also upon experiential factors.

With regard to the dissolution of the Oedipus complex, Freud has expressed two apparently contradictory views in the same volume: (a) "Normally an Oedipus complex should be abandoned or thoroughly changed simultaneously with the termination of early sex life." "As a rule, this transformation is not thorough enough; therefore, during the period of puberty the Oedipus complex may be revived, in which case it is liable to induce dire results." (b) "At puberty, the impulses and object-relations of a child's early years become reanimated and amongst them the emotional ties of the Oedipus complex." (*The Problem of Lay Analyses.*)

Freud is quite sure from clinical findings (including analyses of children) that the child unconsciously desires much more than mere demonstrations of parental affection. Some form of sensual gratification corresponding to the limitations of his "infantile sexuality" is also necessary to him. The usual culmination of the child's (even of the boy's) unconscious Oedipus wish is to give birth to a baby in some vague manner.

With regard to the actually incestuous nature of the child's unconscious desires Freud is willing to admit that the child never surmises the real facts as to the actual physical sex relations, but this ignorance, he thinks, is mitigated by vague deductions based on impressions and observations. Also it is not until puberty that full-blown unconscious incest desires are experienced. At neither stage of development will conscious conflicts arise unless the child becomes aware of the directly sexual aim connected with his "love" for the parent.

To Jung the Oedipus is really a Possession Complex. He gives the very simple explanation that in the early stage of undifferentiated sex both the boy and the girl want the mother, who is felt as a source of delight, and desire to be rid of the father. The element of eroticism gradually increases, however, and the girl begins to develop a typical affection for the father with a corresponding jealous attitude toward the mother.

The Oedipus Complex is regarded as "such an important thing that the manner in which one enters and leaves it cannot be without its effects." According to Freud's later theories (*The Passing of the Oedipus Complex*) this complex succumbs in the boy to castration fear, that is, his attention and interest become narcistically centered upon the penis and there develop in his Ucs fears of being robbed of it by the father. The castration complex by its threatening attitude "literally smashes to pieces the Oedipus Complex."

For the boy the normal dissolution of the Oedipus Complex is as follows: The unconscious Ego under pressure of castration fear renounces or represses one part of the "incestuous" strivings, desexualizes or sublimates another part, while the rest of the libidinal stream moves on to its final zone-localization at the late genital (or pubertal) stage of development. The boy should now (at the end of the Infancy Period) feel for the mother only sublimated love or tender affection. The hostility toward the father should drop out with the relinquishing of the rivalry between them and there follows an intensification of the primary identification with the father. Concurrently there should be a breaking-up of the Inverted Oedipus through sublimation of the incestuous (homosexual) father-love and a weakening of the primary mother-identification. This outcome consolidates the boy's masculinity. During the Latency Period, the sublimated or desexualized affection should be extended first to the father and gradually to others in the immediate environment beside the parents.

The above is the normal passing of the Oedipus Complex. It may be, however, that the Id will cling very tenaciously to its "incestuous" aims and that the unconscious Ego may fail in its attempts at sublimation. In such a case, fixations will occur and an undue amount of repression will be demanded. This, of course, prepares the way for later neurotic developments. Should the primary identification with the mother involved in the Inverted Oedipus be strengthened instead of weakened, homosexual trends are likely to develop.

At puberty, even in the normal individual, there is a re-enactment

43

Jung sees in Freud's incest desire only a symbolic expression on the infantile level of the desire to return to the original source of life, to the arms of the mother for rest, or to the maternal womb for rebirth. In this sense, according to Hinkle, the Oedipus finds an important place in Jung's philosophy. "The conflict of man lies in the struggle between these two states—the lure of the desire for oneness with the mother versus the desire and need for separate life and development."

Rank agrees with Jung's concept of the Oedipus complex as a "re-birth phantasy," but, in working out this complicated situation (for the boy alone), bases the unconscious sexual wish upon his birth trauma anxiety theory. The mother's body, specifically her genital apparatus, was an object surcharged at his birth with anxiety and fear for the child. The latter now unconsciously senses the opportunity to transform the original source of pain to a source of pleasure, but any attempt to do this is doomed to failure, not only on account of the immaturity of the child, but also "chiefly because the attempt is made upon the primal object itself, with which the entire anxiety and repression of the primal trauma is directly connected."

In one of his more recent writings, Freud says, "As regards what precedes the Oedipus complex in boys, we are far from complete clarity. We know that this prehistoric period includes an identification of an affectionate sort with the boy's father, an identification which is still free from any sense of rivalry in regard to his mother."

Freud believes that masturbation "is attached to the Oedipus complex and serves as a discharge for the sexual excitation belonging to it." He is not clear, however, as to whether the masturbation "has this character from the first, or whether, on the other hand, it makes its first appearance spontaneously as an 'organ activity' and is only brought into relation with the Oedipus complex at some later date." On the whole, he is inclined to think that this second possibility is the more probable.

Whether enuresis sometimes may not be a result of masturbation, and parental attempts at its suppression regarded by boys as a threat of castration, Freud says is also a doubtful question.

of the Oedipus drama. Again there should remain only sublimated or tender affection for the parents. The rest of the libido, its sexual and desexualized aims merging together, should begin to be directed to an exogamous love-object, and "emancipation" from the parent thus be established. Fixations, however, in greater or lesser degree, are likely to occur and influence both later objectchoice and the mental health in general.

In the case of the *girl* the development of the Oedipus situation is quite different. Freud says that from his experience he is inclined to believe that it is "far simpler, less equivocal" than in the case of the boy. At the same time, however, he admits that the elements entering into the rise and fall of the Oedipus Complex in the girl are very shadowy and vague. Rather tentatively he suggests that the Oedipus development may take the following pattern: Her sexual curiosity leads the girl to the discovery of the anatomical differences between herself and her little brothers and boy playmates and "penis envy" develops. Normally she then comes to regard her lack of a penis as castration and her Oedipus Complex begins to develop. This means that having, as in the case of the boy, taken the mother as her love-object the girl's libido must now slip into a new position and take the father as love-object. Phylogenetic factors may bring this about, but it is also believed that the girl's new object-love is the result of an attempt at compensation for the loss of the penis, which is possible because in the unconscious "penis" has symbolically the same value as "child." Thus the girl's Oedipus Complex culminates "in a desire which is long cherished to be given a child by her father as a present, to bear him a child." At the same time feelings of hostility and rivalry develop toward the mother, leading to ambivalence and conflict.

The dissolution of the Oedipus in the girl takes place much more slowly and gradually than in the case of the boy. Freud thinks that it comes about partly because the wish for a child is never fulfilled and partly because of external intimidation in connection with masturbation (threats of loss of love). However, both the wish for

Analysis has revealed that the observations of parental coitus are often responsible for the child's first sexual excitation, and may act as "a starting point for the child's whole sexual development." Freud says that masturbation "together with the two attitudes in the Oedipus complex, later on become attached to this impression, the child having subsequently interpreted its meaning." He is willing to admit, however, that, though a common experience, the observation of coitus is not a universal occurrence, and "so at this point we are faced with the problem of 'primal phantasies.' "

Freud concludes, "Thus, the history of what precedes the Oedipus complex, even in boys, raises all these questions to be sifted and explained; and there is the further problem of whether we are to suppose that the process invariably follows the same course, or whether a great variety of different preliminary stages may not converge upon the same final situation." (*Anatomical Distinction Between the Sexes.*)

Rickman describes the Oedipus complex as being in full force at the phallic stage. It follows the anal-sadistic organization of which ambivalence is such an outstanding characteristic, and thus "inherits an already established fusion of Ego and libidinal impulses toward each parent." The boy experiences erotic genital desires for the mother which cannot come to expression because of the interference of the father. He is unable to put up a fight because of (1) affectionate feelings for the father, (2) physical weakness, (3) fear of danger to his genitals if he gives any expression to his erotic desire for the mother. The conflict must be solved "in such a way that the Ego may undergo as little danger as possible and yet afford the libido as much gratification as possible. The way out of the difficulty involves alterations in object relationship to father and mother and in libido organization."

When the father is perceived to be an obstacle, the full Oedipus complex has developed. The outcome is determined by the relative strength of the masculine and feminine disposition.

The relation to the mother suffers only one change—the renunciation of the phallic mode of pleasure-finding. This is not the same as the complete deflection of libido because some gratification is possible through aim-inhibited relationships. When the mature genital aim emerges, there is liberty given but it must be exogamous.

a penis (Castration Complex) and the wish for a child continue "powerfully charged with libido in the unconscious and help to prepare the woman's nature for its subsequent sex rôle."

H. Deutsch out of her experience in analysis of women believes she has been able to clarify the various steps in the development and decline of the girl's Oedipus Complex. The girl, according to her, passes through two phallic phases; in the first, there is clitoris pleasure and masturbatory practices, but when she discovers her lack of penis she interprets this as punishment for masturbation and develops a sense of guilt. During the second phase there is a transference of this sense of guilt to the incestuous wishes which have developed in connection with the father, and it is this which brings about for the girl the dissolution of her Oedipus Complex.

Freud says the Oedipus Complex is "nuclear" for personality development. On the manner of its dissolving, more than on anything else, depends the determination of later normality or neuroticism. "If the Ego does not achieve much more than a repression of the complex, then the latter persists unconsciously in the Id and will express itself later in some pathogenic effect." Alexander says that an Oedipus fixation, namely, an unsatisfactorily resolved Oedipus, means that the individual "will treat every subsequent love relation as if it were the old incest wish." Then a sense of guilt will attach itself to normal adult sexual expression, causing excessive instinct-restrictions and inhibitions, and, in extreme cases, symptom-formation.

Much normal cultural and creative activity is traceable, according to psychoanalysts, to the Oedipus Complex and it is also, they claim, through formation of the Super-ego the final source of all religion and morality. Such sexual and social aberrations as homosexual and some criminal trends also have their origin in this all-critical experience.

The Oedipus experience results, among other things, in the establishment of what Freud calls "conditions of love," that is, the future choice of an object, and the behavior with respect to the object will always be determined to some extent by certain

Klein believes she has sufficient data to establish the existence of a femininity phase in the early sexual development, which, in the boy, becomes a Femininity Complex (or Inferiority Complex). This occurs at the anal-sadistic level and its favorable issue is of great importance for the later development.

The boy is believed during his femininity phase to feel frustrated, just as does the girl during her masculinity phase, because of the lack of a special organ. He identifies with the mother and covets the vagina and breasts as organs of receptivity and bounty. He also equates feces with child, and desires to have children. His anal sadism and destructive tendencies become predominantly directed towards the organs of conception, pregnancy and parturition; he wants to rob the mother of the womb and its contents, viz. children and the penis of the father which he believes to be in the womb. As a result of the hostile impulses towards the mother he fears punishment (mutilation and dismemberment) from, her, and interprets the anal frustrations in this way. "In terms of psychic reality the mother is already the castrator" and the way is also paved for the Castration Complex.

This dread of the mother as castrator may seriously interfere with the normal development of the boy's Oedipus situation. The outcome largely depends on the strength of the constitutional genitality. The struggle between the genital and pre-genital positions of the libido may end in regression to or fixation in pre-genital sadism and mother identification and will show itself later in an attitude of marked rivalry towards women, a blending of envy and hatred. Klein points out that the establishment of the genital position of the libido prompts to rivalry with men but this is not normally of the asocial nature which it shows in connection with women.

The boy's desire for a child may, with the awakening of his epistemophilic impulse (and also because of the recognition which he realizes the girl gives to his superior possession of a penis), lead to a compensatory displacement resulting in a narcistic over-valuation of the penis and an attitude of intellectual rivalry with women.

"A tendency to excess in the direction of aggression which very frequently occurs has its source in the femininity-complex." That is, as Klein says, such aggressive tendencies are rooted in the dread of the mother, though in part also they may be conditioned by over-compensatory attempts to mask sexual ignorance and anxiety, and may also be a unconscious impressions left by the experience. Normally, there will remain only a few traces which point unmistakably to a parental prototype behind the object-choice and behavior; Freud gives as an example of this the preference often shown by younger men for mature women. However, as he says, there are many "strange ways" of loving, and the peculiar conditions of love which underlie them, and to which they owe their characteristics, can always be derived from a fixation in some phase of the Oedipus situation. In this connection, he has established for the man several types of object relationship. These are:

1. The need for "an injured third party" type of object-choice—the man always chooses a woman to whom some other man (brother, husband, lover) has a right of possession. This relates back to the child's concept of the mother as belonging inseparably to the father, and at the same time "the unique, the irreplaceable one." With this type, Freud says, there will often be a series of object-choices, each one of which is really a mother surrogate. The urgent desire in the unconscious "for some irreplaceable thing often resolves itself into an endless series in actuality—endless for the very reason that the satisfaction longed for is in spite of all never found in the surrogate."

2. The need for the "light woman" type of object-choice—that is, for a woman who is "more or less sexually discredited, whose fidelity and loyalty admit of some doubt." Lovers of this type always demand that feelings of jealousy shall be associated with their object-love. The lover himself must fulfill certain conditions of love in his attitude towards his object—he must want to rescue her. This type of object relationship can be traced back, Freud thinks, to an unconscious fixation on the mother first as the ideal and personification of non-sexual purity, with subsequent destruction of this illusion through sexual enlightenment. Or during his Oedipus experience, the boy regards the mother as having been unfaithful to him because of what she has granted to the father. During puberty his revived unconscious Oedipus phantasies center about

protest against the feminine rôle which castration would involve. Klein also speaks of possibilities for sublimation of the "desire for a child and the feminine component which play so essential a part in men's work."

Klein points out that the femininity phase is bound, through the mother-identification, to have some effect upon the Super-ego formation in the boy. Like the girl he will make "both cruelly primitive and kindly identifications. But he passes through this phase to resume . . . identification with the father. However much the maternal side makes itself felt in the formation of the super-ego, it is yet the paternal super-ego which from the beginning is the decisive influence for the man. He too sets before himself a figure of an exalted character upon which to model himself, but, because the boy is 'made in the image' of his ideal, it is not unattainable. This circumstance contributes to the more sustained and objective creative work of the male."

Of the "penis-envy" phase in girls Freud writes, "From the analyses of many neurotic women we have learned that women go through an early phase in which they envy their brothers the token of maleness and feel themselves handicapped and ill-treated on account of the lack of it (really, on account of its diminished form). . . . During this early phase little girls often make no secret of their envy of the favorite brother and the animosity it gives rise to against him; they even try to urinate standing upright like the brother, thus asserting the equality with him that they claim."

Of the part played by the Oedipus complex in bringing about a neurosis, Freud writes, "Distinct traces are probably to be found in most people of an early partiality . . . on the part of a daughter for her father or on the part of a son for his mother; but it must be assumed to be more intense from the very first in the case of those children whose constitution marks them down for a neurosis, who develop prematurely and have a craving for love."

the mother's infidelity; "the lover with whom the mother commits the act of unfaithfulness almost invariably bears the features of the boy himself, or to be more correct, of the idealized image he forms of himself as brought to equality with his father by growing to manhood." His later choice of a woman inclined to fickleness and unfaithfulness is due to the fact that these propensities bring her into dangerous situations, "so it is natural that the lover should do all he can to protect her by watching over her virtue and opposing her evil ways."

I

The Symbolic Representation of the Pleasures and Reality Principles in the Oedipus Myth [1]

SCHOPENHAUER writes:[2] "Every work has its origin in a happy thought, and the latter gives the joy of conception; the birth, however, the carrying out, is, in my own case at least, not without pain; for then I stand before my own soul, like an inexorable judge before a prisoner lying on the rack, and make it answer until there is nothing left to ask. Almost all the errors and unutterable follies of which doctrines and philosophies are so full seem to me to spring from a lack of this probity. The truth was not found, not because it was unsought, but because the intention always was to find again instead some preconceived opinion or other, or at least not to wound some favourite idea, and with this aim in view subterfuges had to be employed against both other

[1] Published in Imago, 1912.
[2] Letter to Goethe, dated November the 11th, 1815.

people and the thinker himself. *It is the courage of making a clean breast of it in face of every question that makes the philosopher. He must be like Sophocles' Oedipus, who, seeking enlightenment concerning his terrible fate, pursues his indefatigable enquiry, even when he divines that appalling horror awaits him in the answer. But most of us carry in our hearts the Jocasta, who begs Oedipus for God's sake not to enquire further; and we give way to her, and that is the reason why philosophy stands where it does.*[3] Just as Odin at the door of hell unceasingly interrogates the old prophetess in her grave, disregarding her opposition and refusals and prayers to be left in peace, so must the philosopher interrogate himself without mercy. This philosophical courage, however, which is the same thing as the sincerity and probity of investigation that you attribute to me, does not arise from reflection, cannot be wrung from resolutions, but is an inborn trend of the mind."

The deep and compressed wisdom of these remarks deserves to be discussed, and to be compared with the results of psycho-analysis.

What Schopenhauer says about the psychical attitude requisite for scientific (philosophical) production sounds like the application of Freud's formula about the "principles of psychical happenings"[4] to

---

[3] Not underlined in the original.
[4] Freud. Jahrb. d. Psychoanalyse, Bd. III, S. 1.

the theory of Science. Freud distinguishes two such principles: the pleasure-principle, which in the case of primitive beings (animals, children, savages), as in that of the more primitive mental states (in dreams, wit, phantasy, neurosis, psychosis) plays the leading part and allows processes to come about that only strive for the shortest way of gaining pleasure, while the psychical activity of acts that might create feelings of unpleasantness (*Unlust*) is withdrawn (repression); then the reality-principle, which presupposes a higher development and growth of the psychical apparatus, and has as its characteristic that "in place of the repression, which excluded a number of the incoming ideas as creative of unpleasantness (*Unlust*), impartial judgment appears, which has to decide whether a given idea is true or false, *i. e.* in harmony with reality or not, and which decides by comparison with the memory-traces of reality."

Only one kind of thought activity remains free from the tests of reality, even after the inauguration of the higher principle, and subject solely to the pleasure-principle, namely, phantasy, while it is Science that is most successful in overcoming the pleasure-principle.[5]

Schopenhauer's opinion, quoted above, on the mental disposition requisite for scientific activity would therefore run somewhat as follows if converted into

[5] Freud. Loc. cit., S. 4.

Freud's terminology: the thinker may (and should) give his phantasy play, so as to be able to taste the "joy of conception"—new ideas are of course not to be had in any other way[6]—, but in order that these phantastic notions may evolve into scientific ideas they must first be submitted to a laborious testing by reality.

Schopenhauer recognised with acute perception that the greatest resistances raised against unprejudiced testing of reality, even in the case of a scientist, are not of an intellectual, but of an affective nature. Even the scientist has human failings and passions: vanity, jealousy, moral and religious bias tending to blind him to a truth that is disagreeable to him; and he is only too inclined to regard as true an error that fits his personal system.

Psycho-analysis can only complement Schopenhauer's postulate in a single point. It has found that the inner resistances may be fixed in the earliest childhood and may be completely unconscious; it therefore demands of every psychologist who enters on the study of the human mind that he should thoroughly investigate beforehand his own mental constitution—·inborn and acquired—down to the deepest layers and with all the resources of the analytic technique.

Unconscious affects, however, may falsify the truth not only in psychology, but also in all other

[6] See on this point Robitschek, "Symbolisches Denken in der chemischen Forschung," Imago, Jahrg. I, Heft 1.

sciences, so we have to formulate Schopenhauer's postulate as follows: Everyone who works in Science should first submit himself to a methodical psycho-analysis.

The advantages that would accrue to Science from this deepened self-knowledge on the part of the scientist are evident. An enormous amount of power for work, which is now wasted on infantile controversies and priority disputes, could be put at the disposal of more serious aims. The danger of "projecting into Science as a generally valid theory peculiarities of one's own personality" (Freud [7]) would be much less. The hostile manner also in which, even nowadays, new unusual ideas or scientific propositions are received when put forward by unknown authors, unsupported by any authoritative personality, would give way to a more unprejudiced testing by reality. I will go so far as to maintain that, if this rule of self-analysis were observed, the development of the various sciences, which today is an endless series of energy-wasting revolutions and reactions, would pursue a much smoother, yet a more profitable and an accelerated course.

It cannot be regarded as chance that the Oedipus myth immediately occurred to Schopenhauer when he wished to illustrate by a simile the correct psychical attitude of the scientist in mental production and the

[7] Freud. "Ratschläge, etc." Zentralbl. f. Psychoanalyse, Jahrg. II.

inner resistances that arise against this correct way of working. Had he been—as we analysts are—convinced of the strict determination and determinability of *every* psychical act, this thought would surely have made him reflect. For us, who are the fortunate possessors of the Freudian psychology (which like a mental Dietrich provides a ready key to so many locks that have till now been considered impossible to open), it is not at all difficult to retrieve this piece of analysis. This idea that occurred to Schopenhauer indicates his unconscious perception of the fact that of all inner resistances by far the most significant is the resistance against the infantile fixation on hostile tendencies against the father and on incestuous ones towards the mother.

These tendencies, which through the civilised education of the race and of the individual have become intensely disagreeable, and have therefore been repressed, draw with them into the repression a large number of other ideas and tendencies associated with these complexes, and exclude them from the free interchange of thought, or at all events no longer allow them to be treated with scientific objectivity.

The "Oedipus complex" is not only the nuclear complex of the neuroses (Freud); the kind of attitude adopted towards it also determines the most important character traits of the normal man, and in part also the greater or lesser objectivity of the scientist. A man of science who is prevented by the

incest barrier from admitting to himself nascent inclinations of love and disrespect towards blood-re-
lations will—so as to assure the repression of these
inclinations—also not want, nor be able, to test
in their reality with the impartiality demanded by
Science the actions, works, and thoughts of other
authorities as well as the paternal one.

To decipher the feeling and thought content that
lies behind the wording of the Oedipus myth was thus
beyond even the power of a Schopenhauer, otherwise
so discerning. He overlooked the fact—as did the
whole civilised world until Freud—that this myth is
a distorted wish phantasy, the projection of repressed wish-excitations (father-hate, mother-love)
with an altered pleasure-prefix (abhorrence, shudder-
ing awe) on to an external power, "fate." This re-
construction of the real meaning of the myth, its interpretation as a "material phenomenon" (Silberer),
was thus alien to the philosopher. While writing this
letter he was himself dominated—so I believe—by affects that would have debarred this insight.

The actual occasion that led Schopenhauer to
chose this comparison of himself with Oedipus may be
divined from the other parts of the letter. The neglected philosopher saw himself recognised for the
first time by a man of Goethe's greatness and standing. He answered him with expressions of gratitude
that we are not accustomed to from the proud, self-
confident Schopenhauer: "Your Excellency's kind

letter has given me great pleasure, because everything coming from you is for me of inestimable value, a sacred possession. Further, your letter contains the praise of my work, and your approval outweighs in my estimation that of any other."

That sounds absolutely like the enthusiastic gratitude of one man to an older respected one in whom he hopes to find the long-sought protector, *i. e.* to find again the father. Besides God, King, and national heroes, heroes of the spirit like Goethe are also "*revenants*" of the father for countless men, who transfer to them all the feelings of gratitude and respect that they once shewed to their bodily father. The subsequent quotation of the Oedipus myth, however, may well have been an unconscious reaction against this—perhaps rather extravagant—expression of gratitude towards the father, a reaction that allowed some display of the hostile tendencies that go to make up the fundamentally ambivalent feeling-attitude of a son towards his father. In favour of this view speaks the fact that towards the end the letter becomes more and more proud and self-confident. Schopenhauer there asks Goethe to secure the publication of his chief work (Die Welt als Wille und Vorstellung), and now speaks to him as to an equal; he lays a eulogising emphasis on the unusual value of his book, the remarkable nature of its contents, and the beauty of its style, closing with a few cool, business-like lines, which might perhaps be called

brusque. "I will ask you please to give me a quite
decisive answer without delay, because in case you do
not accept my proposal I will commission someone
who is going to the Leipsic fair to seek a publisher
there for me."

Perhaps it was just the aid of the attention that
had been deviated from the concrete meaning that
enabled Schopenhauer to decipher in this letter the
"functional symbolism" (which for some time escaped
even psycho-analysts) of certain details of the Oedipus myth.

Silberer gives the name of functional symbol-
phenomena to those pictures occurring in dreams,
phantasies, myths, etc., in which not the content of
thought and imagination, but the way of functioning of the mind (*e. g.* its ease, difficulty, inhibition,
etc) is indirectly represented.[8]

If we allow Schopenhauer's comparison and trans-
late it into analytical-scientific language, we have to
say that the two chief personages of Sophocles' tragedy also symbolise the two principles of mental activity. Oedipus, "who, seeking enlightenment concerning his terrible fate, pursues his indefatigable enquiry, even when he divines that appalling horror
awaits him in the answer," represents the reality-
principle in the human mind, which permits none of
the emerging ideas, even those that produce pain, to

[8] Cp. Silberer's throughout original and pregnant works on
symbolism. especially those in the Jahrb. d. Psychoanalyse, Bd.
I-III.

be repressed, but bids all to be equally tested as to their intrinsic truth. Jocasta, "who begs Oedipus for God's sake not to enquire further," is the personification of the pleasure-principle, which, regardless of objective truth, wants nothing else than to spare the ego pain, to gain pleasure wherever possible, and, so as to reach this goal, bans to the unconscious whenever possible all ideas and thoughts that threaten to set free pain.

Encouraged by Schopenhauer's interpretation and its striking analytical confirmation, I venture to go a step further and to raise the question whether it is pure chance that in both the Oedipus myth and the Edda Saga, also cited by our philosopher, the reality-principle is represented by men (Oedipus, Odin) and the pleasure-principle by women (Jocasta, Erda). The psycho-analyst is not accustomed to fly hastily to the idea of "accident," and would incline rather to attribute to the Greek and Teutonic peoples, as well as to Sophocles and Schopenhauer, an unconscious knowledge of the bisexuality of every human being. Schopenhauer actually says that most human beings carry in them Oedipus and Jocasta. In accord with this interpretation is the observation of daily experience that in general in women the tendency to repression—the pleasure-principle, therefore—prevails; in men the capacity for objective judgment and for tolerating painful insight—the reality-principle, therefore.

An eye made keen by individual-psychological experience will certainly be able to discover and solve many more significant symbols in Sophocles' tragedy. I will only point out two very striking ones, both of the category of "somatic symbol-phenomena" (Silberer), in which, therefore, bodily states are mirrored. To start with, there is the name of the tragic hero Oedipus, which in Greek means "swell-foot." This apparently senseless and odd denomination at once loses this character when we know that in dreams and jokes, as well as in the fetishistic worship of the foot or in the neurotic dread of this member, it symbolises the male organ.

The fact that this member is described in the hero's name as swollen is sufficiently explained by its erectibility. It cannot surprise us, by the way, that the myth completely identifies with a phallus the man who achieved the monstrous feat of sexual intercourse with the mother, a feat no doubt conceived as superhuman.

The other somatic symbol-phenomenon is Oedipus' self-blinding as a punishment for his unconscious committed sins. It is true that the tragedian gives the explanation for this punishment: "For why was I to see, When to descry no sight on earth could have a charm for me?" [9] he makes Oedipus (not quite unequivocally) cry out. But certain psycho-analytical

* (I quote throughout from Sir George Young's translation of the Oedipus Tyrannus. Transl.)

62

experiences, in which the eyes regularly have to be interpreted as symbols of the genital organs, give me the right to interpret the self-blinding as a displacement of the really intended self-castration of Oedipus, the talion punishment more comprehensible in this connection. To the horrified question of the Chorus, however;

Rash man, how could'st thou bear to outrage so
Thine eyes? What Power was it, what wrought on
    thee?

the hero answers:

        Apollo, Apollo fulfils,
        O friends, my measure of ills
        Fills my measure of woe.

In other words, it was the sun (Phoebus Apollo), the most typical father-symbol;[10] the hero was no longer to look him in the eyes, a consideration that may have given a second determining factor for the distortion of the castration punishment to blinding.[11]

[10] Freud. "Nachtrag zur Analyse Schrebers," Jahrb. d. Psychoanalyse, Bd. III.

[11] These symbol interpretations will be at once evident to the practised psycho-analyst, since he can find them confirmed in his dream analyses countless times. While reading through this article, however, I received from Dr. Otto Rank the information that the correctness both of the interpretation of the name Oedipus here attempted and that of the sexual-symbolic explanation of self-binding could be determined with certainty from comparative mythological studies. In his work that has just appeared, "Das Inzest-motiv in Dichtung und Sage," these interpretations are substantiated with a rich collection of facts, which makes it possible for the non-analyst also to accept them.

If we have once assimilated these interpretations, it must amaze us to see how the folk-soul should have managed to fuse together in this myth the knowledge (distorted, it is true) of the most significant content, the nuclear complex of the unconscious (*i. e.* the parental complex), with the most general and comprehensive formula of mental activity. Our amazement gives way to understanding, however, when we have learnt from Otto Rank's fundamental mytho-psychological works to grasp the way in which the creative folk-soul works. Rank shewed in a beautiful example [12] that the individual poet "by means of his own complex-tones succeeds in clarifying and emphasising certain attributes of a transmitted material," but that the so-called folk-productions are also to be regarded as the work of numerous or countless individuals, who originate, transmit, and decorate the tradition. "Only in this case," he says further, "the story goes through a series of similarly disposed individual minds, each of which works in the same direction, at the production of general human motives and the polishing of many disturbing accessory works."

After the double interpretation of the Oedipus myth we may imagine the crystallising process of our myth, described by Rank, somewhat as follows:

Significant but unconscious psychical contents

[12] Rank. "Der Sinn der Griselda-Fabel," Imago. Jahrg. I, Heft 1.

(aggressive phantasies against the father, sexual hunger for the mother with erection-tendencies, dread lest the father would avenge the sinful intent with the punishment of castration) procured, each for itself, indirect symbolic representatives in the consciousness of all men. Men with special creative capacities, poets, give expression to these universal symbols. In this way the mythical motives of exposure by the parents, victory over the father, unconscious intercourse with the mother, and self-blinding, might have arisen in individuals independent of one another. In the course of the passage of the myths through countless poetic individual minds, one that Rank has made probable, condensation of the separate motives led secondarily to a greater unity, which then proved to be durable and which was fashioned anew in much the same form by all peoples and at all times.[18]

It is probable, however, that in this, as also in every other myth, and perhaps indeed with mental productivity in general, parallel with the tendency to give expression to psychical contents there is also an unconscious aim at bringing to presentation the mental ways of functioning that are operative in mastering these contents.[14] Only this latter fusion then

[18] See on this point Rank, Der Mythus von der Geburt des Helden (Schriften zur angewandten Seelenkunde, Heft V).

[14] Silberer, to whom we owe the formulation of the idea of functional symbolism, cites a long series of myths and fairy-tales that can be resolved into both material and functional symbol-phenomena. ("Phantasie und Mythos," Jahrb. d. Psychoanalyse, Bd. II.)

yields the perfected myth, which without foregoing
any of its effect on men is transmitted unchanged
for hundreds of years. So was it with the Oedipus
myth, in which not only the most deeply repressed
feeling and thought complexes of mankind are represented in images, but also the play of the mental
forces that were operative in the attempt to master
these contents, differing according to sex and indi-
viduality.

For the correctness of this interpretation let some
passages from the tragedy itself bear witness:

> *Oedipus*: And how can I help dreading
> My mother's bed?
> *Jocasta*: But why should men be fearful,..
> O'er whom Fortune is mistress, and
> fore-knowledge
> Of nothing sure? *Best take life eas-
> ily,*[15]
> *As a man may.* For that maternal
> wedding,
> Have you no fear; for many men ere
> now
> Have dreamed as much; but he who by
> such dreams
> Sets nothing, has the easiest life of it.

* * * * *

[15] The passages in Italics are not underlined in the original

Jocasta (to OEDIPUS, *who, enquiring after the frightful truth, summons the only witness of the crime)* :

> Why ask who 'twas he spoke of?
> Nay, never mind—never remember it—
> 'Twas idly spoken!

Oedipus :

> Nay, it cannot be
> That having such a clue I should refuse
> To solve the mystery of my parentage!

Jocasta :

> For heaven's sake, if you care for your own life,
> *Don't seek it! I am sick, and that's enough!*

> * * * * *

Jocasta : But I beseech you, hearken! Do not do it!

Oedipus : I will not hearken—not to know the whole.

Jocasta : I mean well; and I tell you for the best!

Oedipus : What you call best is an old sore of mine.

Jocasta : *Wretch, what thou art O might'st thou never know!*

> * * * * *

Oedipus : *Break out what will, I shall not hesitate,*
> *Low though it be, to trace the source of me.*

> * * * * *

Symbolism

Shepherd (who was ordered to kill the new-born Oedipus, but who exposed him to the open):

> O, I am at the horror, now, to speak!
> *Oedipus*: And I to hear. But I must hear—no less.

"The Jocasta in us," as Schopenhauer says, the pleasure-principle, as we express it, wishes thus that a man "should best take life easily, as a man may," that he "set no store by" (suppresses) the things that disturb him, *e. g.* that with the most superficial motivation he should refuse to accord any significance to phantasies and dreams about the death of his father and sexual intercourse with his mother, pay no attention to disagreeable and dangerous talk, not search after the origin of things, but above all it warns a man against recognising who he is.

The reality-principle, however, the Oedipus in the human soul, does not allow the seductions of pleasure to keep him from penetrating into even a bitter or a horrible truth, it estimates nothing so lowly as to be not worth testing, it is not ashamed to seek the true psychological nucleus of even superstitious prophecies and dreams, and learns to endure the knowledge that in the inmost soul aggressive and sexual instincts dwell that do not pause even at the barriers erected by civilisation between the son and his parents.

II

On Eye Symbolism [16]

Relying on psycho-analytical experience, I have tried to interpret Oedipus' self-blinding as a self-castration.[17] I wish here to relate shortly the facts on which I relied for the purpose of this interpretation.

1. A young lady suffered from a phobia of sharp objects, especially needles. Her obsessive fear ran: such an object might sometime put out her eyes. Closer investigation of the case disclosed the fact that the lady had for a number of years lived with her friend in sexual intimacy, but had anxiously guarded against permitting the intermissio penis, which would have impaired her anatomical integrity by rupturing the hymen. All sorts of accidents now kept happening to her, most of which affected the eye; most commonly unintentional self-inflicted injuries with needles. Interpretation: Substitution of the genitals by the eyes, and representation of the wishes and fears relating to the former by accidental actions and phobias relating to the latter.

2. A myopic patient with conscious fears of inferiority and compensating grandiose phantasies transferred all his hypochondriac and anxious feel-

---

[16] Published in the Internat. Zeitschr. f. ärztl. Psychoanalyse, 1913, as a contribution to the symposium on eye symbolism.
[17] See Chapter X, Section 1.

ings, and an exaggerated sense of shame, on to his short-sightedness; these feelings, however, relate in his unconscious to the genitals. When a small child he had sexual "omnipotent phantasies" concerning his mother and sister; latér on painful realisation of his sexual inferiority ("small penis" complex, hypochondria, "states of weakness"), which was compensated for by excesseive onanism and sadistic acts of coitus. With the help of the symbolic equating: eye=genital, he managed to represent by means of the eye a great part of his sexual wishes and fears. An incomplete analytic enlightenment reduced his hypochondria very appreciably.

3. I had the opportunity of getting to know a family whose members suffered without exception from an exaggerated fear of injuries and diseases of the eye. The mere mention of bad or injured eyes made them get pale, and the sight of such things could lead to fainting. In one member of the family the psychical disturbances of potency could be recognised to be the manifestations of masochism which had appeared as a reaction against sadistic desires; the fear of eye injuries was the reaction to the sadistic wish to injure the eye, a displacement of the sadistic coitus wish. It had been very easy for the sadistic-masochistic components of the sexual instinct to be transferred from the genital to another organ susceptible to injury.

Another member of this family extended fear and

disgust for eyes on to corns as well; in this not only the external resemblance and the identity of the name,[18] but a second symbolic equating (toe=penis) played a part. This was evidently an attempt to bring the symbol eye once more nearer to the real thing (genital organ) with the help of a mediate idea (corn).

4. A patient who was afraid of beetles when a child developed at the time of puberty a dread of seeing himself in a mirror, especially of seeing his own eyes and eyebrows. This dread turned out to be on the one hand an auto-perception of his tendency to repression (not wanting to look himself in the eye), on the other hand a representation of the fear of onanism. With the help of the idea of movability the child succeeded in displacing his attention and affects from the spontaneously movable (erectile) organ on to the movable beetle. The beetle's vulnerability also, the way in which even a child can so easily crush it under foot, renders it a suitable object for taking the place of the original object of attack, the sexual organ. A further displacement then set the equally movable and vulnerable eye in place of the beetle. I might also mention that in Hungarian the pupil is designated by a word meaning literally, "eye-beetle."

5. In a whole series of anxiety dreams (mostly

---

[18] (Corns in German are called "Hühneraugen," literally "fowls' eyes." Transl.)

recollected from childhood) eyes figure that grow
alternately larger and smaller. From the total con-
text I have had to regard these eyes as symbols of
the male sexual organ in its changing size (erection).
The apparent change in size of the eyes on opening
and closing the lids is obviously used by the child to
represent genital processes that are accompanied by
changes in size. Children's dread, often excessive, of
their parents' eyes has also, in my opinion, a sexual-
symbolic root.

6. In another series of dreams, eyes (as paired
organs) represent the testicles. Since the face
(apart from the hands) is the only uncovered part
of the body, children have to satisfy all their curiosity relating to other parts of the body on the head
and face of their adult friends, especially the parents. Each part of the face thus becomes the representative of one or more genital areas. The face
is specially well adapted (nose in the middle between the eyes and eyebrows, with the mouth below)
for representation of the penis, testicles, pubic hair,
and anus.

I have no doubt that the sense of embarrassment
one experiences on being stared at, and which keeps
one from staring hard at others, finds its explanation in the sexual-symbolic significance of the parts
of the face. This must also go to explain the marked
effect of the hypnotiser's eyes on his medium. I may
refer also to the sexual symbolism in ogling, in the

bashful drooping of the eyes, casting of the eyes on someone, etc., further such expressions as "to cast eyes at someone, to throw sheep's eyes," [19] etc.

7. Finally I may relate the case of an obsessional patient who confirmed subsequently my interpretation of Oedipus' self-blinding. As a child he was unusually spoilt, fixed on his parents, but very bashful and modest. One day he learnt from other children the real course of sexual relations between the parents. At this he displayed intense anger at his father, often with the conscious phantasy that he was castrating him (the father), which was always followed, however, by remorse and self-punishment. Now one of these self-punishments was that he destroyed the eyes in his own portrait. I was able to explain to the patient that in doing so he was only expiating in a disguised way the castration he had wished to perform on his father, in accordance with the Mosaic talion threat of punishment, "an eye for an eye, and a tooth for a tooth," which, by the way, takes for example just the two castration symbols, blinding and tooth-extraction.[20]

In a work on the stages in the development of the sense of reality [21] I have attempted to explain the origin of symbolism from the impulse to represent infantile wishes as being fulfilled, by means of the

[19] (Cp. the modern slang expression, "to make a glad eye." Transl.)
[20] See my remarks on tooth-symbolism in Chapter VI.
[21] Chapter VIII.

child's own body. The symbolic identification of external objects with bodily organs makes it possible to find again, on the one hand, all the wished-for objects of the world in the individual's body, on the other hand, the treasured organs of the individual's body in objects conceived in an animistic manner. The tooth and eye symbolism would be examples of the fact that bodily organs (principally the genital ones) can be represented not only by objects of the outer world, but also by other organs of the body. In all probability this is even the more primary kind of symbol-creation.

I imagine that this symbolic equating of genital organs with other organs and with external objects originally happens only in a playful way, out of exuberance, so to speak. The equations thus arising, however, are secondarily made to serve repression, which seeks to weaken one member of the equation, while it symbolically over-emphasises the other, more harmless one by the amount of the repressed affect. In this way the upper half of the body, as the more harmless one, attains its sexual-symbolic significance, and so comes about what Freud calls "Displacement from below upwards." In this work of repression the eyes have proved to be specially adapted to receive the affects displaced from the genital region, on account of their shape and changeable size, their movability, their high value, and their sensitiveness. It is to be supposed, however, that this displacement would not have succeeded so well, had not the eye already had from the beginning that significant libidinous value that Freud describes in his "Sexualtheorie" as a special component of the sexual instinct (the impulse of sexual visual curiosity).

III

The Ontogenesis of Symbols [22]

Dr. Beaurain's remarks [23] about the ways in which the child comes to form its first general concepts can be fully confirmed by whoever has had the opportunity to watch the mental development of the child, either directly, or else indirectly *via* parents whose powers of observation had been psychologically sharpened. There can be no doubt that the child (like the unconscious) identifies two things on the basis of the slightest resemblance, displaces affects with ease from one to the other, and gives the same name to both. Such a name is thus the highly condensed representative of a large number of fundamentally different individual things, which, however, are in some way or other (even if ever so distantly) similar and are for this reason identified. Advance in the knowledge of reality (intelligence) then mani-

[22] Published in the Internat. Zeitschr. f. ärztl. Psychoanalyse, 1913.
[23] Beaurain, "Ueber das Symbol und die psychischen Bedingungen für sein Entstehen beim Kinde," in the same number of the Zeitschrift.

fests itself in the child in the progressive resolution of such condensation-products into their elements, in learning to distinguish from one another things that are similar in one respect but otherwise different. Many writers have already rightly grasped and described this process; Silberer's and Beaurain's communications on the subject have brought further confirmation and have deepened our insight into the details of this development process in the mind.

All these authors see in the infantile inadequacy of the capacity for making distinctions the chief factor in the origination of the ontogenetic and phylogenetic preliminary stages of the knowledge processes.

I should like here to raise an objection only against designating all these preliminary stages in knowledge with the word "Symbol;" similes, allegories, metaphors, allusions, parables, emblems, and indirect representations of every sort might also in a certain sense be conceived as products of this lack of sharpness in distinction and definition, and yet they are not—in the psycho-analytical sense—symbols. Only such things (or ideas) are symbols in the sense of psycho-analysis as are invested in consciousness with a logically inexplicable and unfounded affect, and of which it may be analytically established that they owe this affective over-emphasis to *unconscious* identification with another thing (or idea), to which the surplus of affect really belongs. Not all similes, therefore, are symbols, but only those in which the one member of the equation is repressed into the unconscious.[24] Rank and Sachs conceive a symbol in the same sense.[25] "We understand by this," they say, "a special kind of indirect representation which is distinguished by certain peculiarities from other allied kinds, such as the simile, the metaphor, the allegory, the allusion, and other forms of figurative representation of thought-material (of the rebus variety)," and "it is a substitutive, illustrative replacement-expression for something hidden."

This being so, it is more prudent not to assume that the conditions under which symbols arise are identical with those for analogy-formation in general, but to presuppose for this specific kind of analogy-formation specific conditions of origin, and to search for these.

Now analytical experience shews us in fact that although the condition of intellectual insufficiency has to be fulfilled with the formation of real symbols as well, the chief conditions for their production are not of an intellectual, but of an affective nature. I will demonstrate this with individual examples from sexual symbolism.

So long as the necessities of life do not compel

[24] See on this matter my remarks in earlier articles, Ch. VI, Ch. VIII, Ch. X, Sect. 2, and my review on Jung's Libido essay in the Internat. Zeitschr. f. arztl. Psychoanalyse, Jahrg. I, S. 393.

[25] Rank und Sachs. Die Bedeutung der Psychoanalyse für die Geisteswissenschaften. 1913. S. 11. et seq. . . .

them to adaptation and therewith to the knowledge
of reality, children concern themselves to begin with
only about the satisfaction of their instincts, *i. e.*
about the parts of the body where this satisfaction
takes place, about the objects suited to evoke this,
and about the actions that actually evoke the satisfaction. Of the sexually excitable parts of the body
(erogenous zones), for instance, they are specially
interested in the mouth, the anus, and the genitals.
"What wonder, then, if also his attention is arrested
above all by those objects and processes of the outer
world that on the ground of ever so distant a resemblance remind him of his dearest experiences." [26]
Thus comes about the "sexualisation of everything." [27] In this stage small boys are prone to
apply the childish term for genitals to all long objects, they see an anus in every hole, urine in every
fluid, and faeces in every softish material.

A boy, aged about one and a half, said when he
was first shewn the Danube: "What a lot of spit!"
A two-year-old boy called everything that could
open, a door, including even his parents' legs, since
these can open and shut (be abducted and adducted).

Similar analogies are formed also within the sphere
of the bodily organs themselves: Penis and tooth,
anus and mouth, become equated. Perhaps the child
finds an equivalent in the upper part of the body

[26] Ch. VIII. P. 193.
[27] (A well-known expression of the philologist Kleinpaul.
Transl.)

(especially on the head and face) for every affectively important part of the lower half.

This equating, however, is not yet symbolism. Only from the moment when as the result of cultural education the one member of the equation (the more important one) is repressed, does the other previously less important member attain affective over-significance and become a symbol of the repressed one. Originally penis and tree, penis and church-steeple, were consciously equated; but only with the repression of the interest in the penis do the tree and church-steeple become invested with inexplicable and apparently ungrounded interest; they become penis symbols.

In this way also eyes become symbols of the genitalia, with which they had previously been identified —on the ground of extrinsic resemblance. There thus comes about a symbolic over-emphasis of the upper half of the body in general, after interest in the lower half has been repressed, and all genital symbols that play such an extensive part in dreams (necktie, snake, tooth-drawing, box, ladder, etc.) must have originated ontogenetically in the same way. I should not be surprised if in a dream of the boy mentioned above a door re-appeared as a symbol of the parental lap, and in a dream of the other boy's the Danube as a symbol of bodily fluids.

I desired with these examples to point out the overwhelming significance of affective factors in the production of true symbols. It is they that have to be taken into consideration in the first place when one wishes to distinguish symbols from other psychical products (metaphors, similes, etc.), which are also the result of condensation. One-sided consideration of formal and rational conditions in the explanation of psychical processes can easily lead one astray.

For instance, one was formerly inclined to believe that things are confounded because they are similar; nowadays we know that a thing is confounded with another only because certain motives for this are present; similarity merely provides the opportunity for these motives to function. In the same way it must be said that apperceptive insufficiency alone, without consideration of the motives impelling towards analogy-formation, do not adequately explain the creation of symbols.

THE ŒDIPUS COMPLEX, TRANSFERENCE, AND SUBLIMATION

BOTH science and art may, in the Freudian view, show evidence of the working of the Œdipus complex in sublimated form. Scientific curiosity may sometimes be a redirection of repressed sexual curiosity, a curiosity which the child feels to be wrong and in need of repression. I recall the case of an individual who was being analysed by a leading Freudian. He himself pointed out that his early interests were certainly not in the direction of biological problems at all, but in astronomy and divinity. The confident Freudian interpretation was that that was a projection, and that there had been a repression of interests that were on biological lines. As amounting almost to a proof of this, the analyst pointed out that the constellations in the heavens mythically represent human situations, and said that the patient had turned from the baffling problem of the origin of life in his earliest years and fixed his mind upon the stars, these being as far away as possible; and yet upon these stars man had projected human situations.

I do not know how far that can be taken as representing tendentiousness in the reasoning of a Freudian or as containing a kernel of important truth. Probably both. In the early stages of development of psycho-analytic doctrine deductions are apt to be rather crude, but they do contain a germ of truth, a new point of view which we should all be ready not only to recognize but also to follow up.

THE ŒDIPUS COMPLEX

The Œdipus-complex situation seems a kind of " open sesame " in psycho-analytical literature and even as regards the interpretation of plays and other works of art. I was glancing again through Freud's *Collected Papers* recently and was caught by a few pages he wrote about *Macbeth*.[1] Everything he writes is extremely stimulating and suggestive. At all events it starts the mind working with a new point of view. Freud points out—a fact generally overlooked—how curious it is that although at the beginning Lady Macbeth is the leading figure in the drama, the strong character, remorseless, unpitying, she is the weaker character at the end. When she sees the sleeping Duncan she says :

> " Had he not resembled
> My father as he slept, I had done 't."

It is the resemblance to her own father which checks her murderous impulse. The situation in her mind is the Œdipus complex, the relation to her own father and mother. She breaks down after having apparently achieved her object (see previous chapter). In the end Lady Macbeth is mentally weaker, though still morally stronger, than her husband. "Macbeth does murder sleep." But it is not Macbeth who suffers from sleeplessness.[2] It is Lady Macbeth who suffers from sleeplessness and walks in her

---

[1] " Some Character-Types met with in Psycho-Analytic Work." S. Freud, *Collected Papers*, Vol. IV, pp. 326–33. Hogarth Press, London, 1925.

[2] No doubt he lost some sleep at first, but he did not become a victim of insomnia !

LADY MACBETH : You lack the season of all natures, sleep.
MACBETH : Come, we'll to sleep : my strange and self-abuse
Is the initiate fear, that wants hard use :
We are yet but young in deed.
                              Act III, Sc. 4.

sleep. There is a curious contrast between these two characters. Macbeth says :

> " Will all great Neptune's ocean wash this blood
> Clean from my hand ?
> No : this my hand will rather
> The multitudinous seas incarnadine,
> Making the green one red."

Lady Macbeth, in the same scene, says :

> " A little water clears us of this deed,"

and yet, later on, in the sleep-walking scene, she reveals her subconscious reactions in the well-known words :

> " Here's the smell of the blood still: all the perfumes of Arabia will not sweeten this little hand. Oh! oh! oh!"

Freud suggestively reminds us of the German theory that Shakespeare sometimes represented one personality by two separate dramatic characters. There is some support for that supposition. Macbeth and Lady Macbeth may well be two sides of the same personality. Is that very surprising ? When people are married they become one, and we get one personality—a single personality for many purposes in the eyes of the law, but also a single personality very often from the psychological point of view. If one reads the play *Macbeth* with that in mind it becomes much more instructive. There is a kind of conflict envisaged within the composite personality—a conflict between good and evil, between the more primitive tendencies and the higher ideas. Lady Macbeth originally has great strength of character and shows real love for her husband. Yet she it is who commits suicide in the end. Macbeth, the weaker character at the beginning, refuses to commit suicide. He says, right at the end of the play,

> " Why should I play the Roman fool, and die
> On mine own sword ? whiles I see lives, the gashes
> Do better upon them."

One side of his character has become firm at all events, although, of course, on a very low and primitive level.[1] Macbeth has a far weaker super-ego than has Lady Macbeth. Moreover it is she who says :

> " These deeds must not be thought
> After these ways : so, it will make us mad."

This is the only direct mention of madness in the play.

The childlessness of the two is worth remembering.[2] There is a very significant remark of Macduff, replying to Malcolm, when told of the slaughter of his children :

> " He has no children—All my pretty ones ! "

That again is linked up with the message of the witches. Macbeth is told, " Thou shalt be king hereafter," and yet Banquo is greater than Macbeth because he shall " get kings," though he be none himself. All of which throws one back to the Œdipus complex.

This line of argument may seem loose and tendentious, not scientific, and certainly Shakespeare had no conscious appreciation of the Œdipus complex ; nevertheless his own unconscious well reacted to the story of Macbeth, a story for which Holinshed furnished all the materials. He compressed the action of many years into a few days, and probably coloured it with his own Œdipus complex. One is led to the probability that Shakespeare may himself have suffered from the Œdipus complex, which breaks through right and left as a possible explanation of many

---

[1] Compare the contrasting mental attitudes in the two phases of manic-depressive psychosis (Chapter IV). One is also reminded of C. G. Jung's doctrine of the *animus* and the *anima* in the unconscious of woman and man, respectively.

[2] Although Lady Macbeth had previously had a child. See *Macbeth*, Act I, Sc. 7, ll. 59, 60:

> " I have given suck, and know
> How tender 'tis to love the babe that milks me."

passages in *Hamlet*[1] and in certain of the other plays. Some of the plots are by no means satisfactory, not even psychologically probable, and yet they have kept many generations of audiences fascinated. This cannot be attributed merely to their literary style, rather is it their appeal to the unconscious of the onlookers quite as much as to the conscious. The appeal is all the stronger if it is unwitting.

It must be remembered that the Œdipus complex has many different forms. There are all degrees of reaction in the child to its parents. At one end of the scale the boy is attracted to his mother and hostile to his father ; at the other end he is attracted to his father and hostile to his mother. A great deal of the hostility to the mother that becomes apparent on analysis is a reaction to the opposite situation in the earliest years. Two outstanding historical examples are Schopenhauer in philosophy and Bismarck in politics. Hostility to the father is, of course, much more frequent, and in strong characters it leads to an intensification of ambition and therefore greater success. The case of Julius Cæsar, in whom ambition knew no bounds, has to be taken in relation with the well-founded story that he dreamt that he was sleeping with his mother, and this was interpreted by the soothsayers as a promise that he would possess mother earth.

There is meaning in that, if we take it in the Freudian sense. If we accept the thesis that the very young child may have an overwhelming wish to have the love of the mother to himself and to exclude other people, it may suggest a very strong potential urge showing itself later in the typically ambitious life of the person who kicks away the ladder by which he has ascended and goes on

[1] See Ernest Jones : " The Œdipus-Complex as an Explanation of Hamlet's Mystery : A Study in Motive." *American Journal of Psychology*, Jan., 1910, pp. 72–113.

ruthlessly in an obsessive way in pursuit of what he wants. These ambitious people are not normal. They are under unusual compulsions and obsessions. Like Alexander, they cry for fresh worlds to conquer. They can be distinguished from the normal person, who has ordinary self-respect, resolution, sense of duty, and regard for others.

> " I dare do all that may become a man ;
> Who dares do more, is none."

The Obsessed Individual

The obsessed individual is gripped by unconscious forces which he cannot fully understand or control. One of the great dangers of the present international situation turns upon the characters of outstanding personalities. So far as they can retain insight into their own personal aims and ideals, and can avoid the grip of obsessional and compulsive tendencies, their influence upon world-history may be, on balance, creative and beneficent. If not . . .

This illustrates how psychology is of the utmost importance in human affairs. It is, indeed, of transcendent importance, more so than any other science, if importance can be compared. It is hardly possible for any intelligent person to remain indifferent to psychology in the present international situation. At every turn the psychological fact makes its appearance.

I return to the process of sublimation, which is the central problem for the mature personality. Only through continued sublimation can the personality remain supple, plastic, able to continue to adapt itself to changing circumstances, able to live in the true sense. The personality must advance, otherwise it will fall back. It is in a state of moving equilibrium. Like an aeroplane, it can hover, but if it stands still it crashes. It moves forward by a process of sublimation, finding an outlet for repressed instinctive energies along paths that are of benefit to society and to the race.

It might be said that in sublimation there is no ultimate goal.

New occasions teach new duties ;
Time makes ancient good uncouth.

We can never completely fulfil our duties. Duties are continually developed as our power and opportunities increase. But this ever-growing achievement of the personality is determined by certain general principles of inter-relation of values of the nature of eternal values, whereas the sublimation that occurs in the obsessed personality is too limited and is not checked in that way. Therefore in the case of the obsessed personality, while they achieve fulfilment of their duty to themselves and to their chosen goal, following a vision of some particular kind, other lines of duty tend to be neglected and even ignored.

TRANSFERENCE

Let me add something rather more systematic about sublimation in relation to transference. In dealing with the mature personality who meets with difficulties and needs help, one finds the process of transference very important. Transference is not co-extensive with personal influence. The latter is a wider conception, but it can take place through transference. One individual can influence another through the transference situation. When the psychotherapist is listening to the patient's story of his life, transference may begin. It lends authority to the physician and makes the patient ready to listen to him. But that form of personal relationship should be only a temporary one. It occurs inevitably in the situation of analysis, but it should be eventually cleared up and resolved by tracing back the fixations, etc., to their true source and revealing their true object in early years.

But even when that occurs personal influence does not come to an end. There is such a thing as direct influence of one character upon another. Transference is always occurring, not only in the consulting-room, but in ordinary life. The extent to which it plays a part in ordinary life varies with the individual and the situation. In the case of the psycho-neurotic a great and obvious part is played by transference. The best form of relationship between two persons is one which is purged of transference. That is the relation to which we should all aspire as between friends and between husband and wife. Transference is an element of weakness. It is temporarily helpful and even necessary in psychotherapeutic treatment, but it is an unwitting element, not completely under personal control, it affects the primitive impersonal part of the mind, the *id*, which is going its own way.

It is this element of transference so evident in totalitarian government that disturbs one. So far as the people concerned and their leaders understand themselves fully and have control, the relationship is a good one. They can get all the good possible out of the unification of the State without the evil of being at the mercy of the whim of some particular individual or the victims of his possible self-deception.

Again, the experience of falling in love is often just a transference situation, although it may lead to a happy romance later on. The transference, while it lasts, can introduce gravely misleading elements. It can disguise incompatibility of temperament and other conditions which are to be avoided as prejudicial to a happy marriage. The person who is repeatedly falling in love is a person who is in the situation of transference. I have always felt that Don Juan ought to have been analysed! One of the results of long analysis is to free the individual from momentary fascinations and infatuations. When I mentioned this to some young people a few years ago they exclaimed in horror and made a mental note never to be analysed. Analysis does free a person from these dangers, but it does not mean that he or she cannot, thereafter, fall in love. The transference situation means the projection by one individual of an emotional situation, which, of course, is liable to disappear as quickly as it came, so that the glory is departed and all the fascination is gone. Where has the fascination gone to when the individual falls out of love as quickly as he or she fell in ? It was a projection, and it has gone back to the individual who projected it. It came from within, it was an illusion. An illusion is a sensory or emotional fulfilment of repressed tendencies. It is a disguised form of wish-fulfilment. [Sensory illusions (optical, etc.) are quite different.]

Although, therefore, the transference situation may help sublimation by temporarily enabling the individual to benefit, yet ultimately sublimation must be independent of the transference situation. Further progress in the individual must come from something higher than transference. The influence of a strong personality, with purpose and high ideals, as an incentive and encouragement, is often necessary, but that kind of relationship is distinct from a transference. In holding such a view as that I part company with the Freudians because they consider that psycho-analysis is almost entirely a matter of carrying on the analysis in a systematic way and relieving repressions, but that any direct interference on the part of the analyst is to be deprecated.

I would say, therefore, that the patient should be helped in such a way that the transference situation may exercise its utmost value, but that eventually the patient must be enabled to free himself from transference.[1] There is a further duty incumbent upon the analyst, namely, to give the patient all the help he can in reconstructing his life, building up a philosophy of life, and learning to live, by the aid of direct influence, which is the proper method whereby one person may affect another.

[1] The transference is " resolved " by being traced back to memories and emotional reactions of early childhood, in the course of the analysis.

Lightning Source UK Ltd.
Milton Keynes UK
UKHW04f0609190918
329155UK00001B/126/P